# EVERY SCHOOL

# EVERY SCHOOL

## ONE CITIZEN'S GUIDE TO
## TRANSFORMING EDUCATION

## DONALD P. NIELSEN

SEATTLE      DISCOVERY INSTITUTE PRESS      2019

## Description

How would an entrepreneur reform education? In Every School, Don Nielsen draws on his business career and twenty-five years as a school activist, to offer innovative solutions to the educational challenges facing our country. Lasting change, Nielsen argues, will not come mainly through local school boards, but rather through state legislative action that empowers school administrators to make choices in the interests of their students. The book is essential reading for parents, policymakers and citizens who want to improve the present system, and who have the courage to pursue the recommendations contained within.

## Library Cataloging Data

*Every School: One Citizen's Guide to Transforming Education* by Donald P. Nielsen

254 pages, 6 x 9 x 0.6 inches & 0.8 lb, 229 x 152 x 14 mm. & 0.35 kg

Library of Congress Control Number: 2019936339

ISBN-13 978-1-936599-62-2 (paperback), Kindle ISBN: 978-1-936599-63-9, EPUB ISBN: 978-1-936599-64-6,

BISAC: EDU034000 Education/Educational Policy & Reform/General

BISAC: EDU000000 Education/General

BISAC: EDU001020 Education/Administration/Elementary & Secondary

## Publisher Information

Discovery Institute Press, 208 Columbia Street, Seattle, WA 98104

Internet: http://www.discoveryinstitutepress.com/

Published in the United States of America on acid-free paper.

Second Edition, First Printing, April 2019.

To the thousands of teachers and principals who
achieve amazing results in spite of the system.

And to my wife, Melissa, for tolerating my passion for public
education and for being such a wonderful partner for 59 years.

# Advanced Praise for *Every School*

"Don Nielsen provides unusually clear insight into the complex issues that inhibit high educational attainment of our public school systems. He follows up the diagnosis with a series of feasible and practical recommendations for how to improve our schools. Nielsen's book should be a must-read for anyone interested in public education."

—ALLEN S. GROSSMAN, SENIOR FELLOW, MBA CLASS OF 1957, PROFESSOR OF MANAGEMENT PRACTICE RETIRED, HARVARD BUSINESS SCHOOL

"In what seems to be a reoccurring challenge with each generation, the question remains how we can best address our nation's deficiencies in our K–12 educational system. It is a question that must be answered if we are to achieve our highest potential as a nation and in our children. Don Nielsen provides a thoughtful response. He not only addresses the root causes of our challenges, but provides a framework for how to align P-12 education to achieve greater effectiveness and results—corporately and individually. Don's background as co-founder, President, and Chairman of Hazleton Corporation and as the former President of the Board for the Seattle Public Schools provides a unique and grounded perspective to the solutions he offers."

—DAN MARTIN, PhD, PRESIDENT, SEATTLE PACIFIC UNIVERSITY

"This is an important book—insightful, engaging and anchored in the real problems and opportunities that communities face. Educators, community leaders, and policymakers are fortunate that Don Nielsen has turned his attention and talent to this analysis of contemporary schooling and what we need to do to harness its potential to create responsible citizens. Don is uniquely suited for this role—a community leader, businessman, parent, chair of a large city school board, and informed citizen. The book is practical and revolutionary at the same time and should be on anyone's required reading list if they care about the future of public education."

—ROBERT C. PIANTA, PH.D., DEAN, CURRY SCHOOL OF EDUCATION, UNIVERSITY OF VIRGINIA

# CONTENTS

# PREFACE

PRIOR TO THE ADVENT OF THE COMMON SCHOOL MOST CHILDREN were either schooled at home or in small village schools, "the one room schoolhouse." The level of education of a child depended upon the effort and desire of the parents and on the quality and competency of the community teacher. Families, and the communities they lived in, took on the responsibility of educating the children.

Over time, parents gained more options, including "private benevolent associations, private-venture schools, Latin grammar schools, religious schools, boarding schools and private academies."[1] These early schools, and the home schooling provided by parents, did a pretty good job of educating children.

> Hamilton was twenty in the retreat from New York; Burr was twenty-one; Light Horse Harry Lee, twenty-one… What amounted to a college class rose up and struck down the British Empire, afterwards helping to write the most sophisticated governing documents in modern history.[2]
>
> George Washington had no schooling until he was eleven, no classroom confinement, no blackboards. He arrived at school already knowing how to read, write and calculate about as well as the average college student today. [3]

Not every child was so well-educated as those described above. Many children grew up illiterate and had limited access to learning environments. As the country grew, this became an issue of increasing concern for policy-makers. They could see the industrial revolution take hold in Europe and knew that America had to get ready to participate in this societal change.

In the 1830s, this concern became actionable as the Massachusetts legislature created the country's first Board of Education. To lead this new board, the Governor, in 1837, appointed Horace Mann, a lawyer and former legislator, to be Secretary.

Horace Mann took great interest in his new position and in 1838 began publishing the "Common School Journal," in which he delineated his views on education. His main principles were:

- Citizens cannot maintain both ignorance and freedom;
- Education should be paid for, controlled, and maintained by the public;
- Education should be provided in schools that embrace children from varying backgrounds;
- Education must be nonsectarian;
- Education must be taught under the tenets of a free society;
- Education must be provided by well-trained, professional teachers.[4]

With these principles in mind, he set about to establish a system of schools for Massachusetts. He felt that all children, regardless of their life circumstances, should receive a good education. While in office, he traveled to Europe to study school systems there. In Prussia (now a part of Germany), he found what he was looking for. King Frederick the Great of Prussia had set up a system of tax-supported schools designed to provide an eight-year course, from age six to fourteen, of compulsory education for all children. The Prussian schools provided not only the skills needed in an early industrialized world, (reading, writing, and arithmetic), but also provided a strict education in ethics, duty, discipline, and obedience.

> Focusing on following directions, basic skills, and conformity, he [King Frederick] sought to indoctrinate the nation from an early age. Isolating students in rows and teachers in individual classrooms fashioned in strict hierarchy—intentionally fostering fear and loneliness.[5]
>
> Mann chose the Prussian model, with its depersonalized learning and strict hierarchy of power, because it was the cheapest and easiest way to teach literacy on a large scale.[6]

Massachusetts adopted this system and became the first state to provide access to a free public education for all of its citizens. Over the next 66 years, every other state made the same guarantee. The result was a publicly funded system where, in every American classroom, groups of about 28 students of roughly the same age were taught by one teacher, usually in an 800 square-foot room. This model has been the dominant archetype ever since.[7]

By the early years of the twentieth century, all states had adopted compulsory education, along with child labor laws that prevented children from being hired for factory employment.

In his 1919 *Public Education in the United States*, Ellwood P. Cubberley suggested that modern life had deprived children of the training that life in farms and villages had once provided, so public schools must take up the task of preparing them for industry and society.[8]

As the country grew, and immigrants began to flood the nation, school populations dramatically increased. The Great Depression, in concert with enacted child labor laws, caused another major increase in school attendance.

The 1920's provided the initial burst in high school attendance, but the Great Depression added significantly to high school enrollment and graduation rates.[9]

High school, not college, was the predominant educational attainment during the first half of the twentieth century. Increased high school graduation rates created a work force ideal for the manufacturing boom that was occurring. A school system that treated students like raw material and treated them to a uniform education created a workforce perfectly designed for the production-line job. However, "as late as 1950, only 25 percent of black students and 50 percent of white students remained in high school long enough to earn a diploma."[10]

The original Prussian school system selected a few students to go on to higher education, with the balance being educated to a level that would allow them to work in the factories or on the farm. Our school system did the same.

The factory model of education is still with us today. That model was, and still is, designed to effectively educate all children to a certain level and allow a few to rise to advanced levels. Today, as in decades past, our schools effectively educate about 25–30 percent of our students, another 45–50 percent graduate with limited skills that do not prepare them for the world of work, and 20–25 percent drop out prior to graduation. This has been the case for decades. I would argue that this performance is designed into the system and that we cannot change the outcome without changing the system.

Prior to the early 1960s, this type of performance was acceptable. Our economy was largely a manufacturing and agricultural economy and those who entered the work force needed only a rudimentary level of reading, writing, and mathematical skills. In the first half of the twentieth century, except during the Depression, a person with limited skills could still find a living-wage job, could buy a house, and raise a family. In fact, in my high school class of 1956, a majority of my peers did not go on to college, but rather went into the job market, and most have lived a very comfortable life.

That environment started to change in the late fifties and early sixties. Manufacturing started to decline and the service economy started to expand. Over the next fifty to sixty years, our manufacturing-based economy was transformed into an information-based and service-based one; and recently, I would argue, it has become an internet-driven economy, as businesses can literally become a global enterprise from the get-go. As all of these changes have occurred, the level of skills and education needed in the American job market has dramatically increased.

Numerous other changes in our society have affected our schools. These are delineated in Chapter 2, but suffice it to say, today's society is totally different from the society of the early twentieth century and even very different from what I faced when I graduated from high school.

With this change, have come increased demands on the educational proficiency that our children need in order to live a comfortable life in the twenty-first century.

Yet during the last sixty years, our schools have operated much as they did in the early twentieth century, even though there have been literally hundreds of reform efforts attempted. What we have witnessed is an institution that is very resistant to change.

Students continue to attend school for six hours per day for approximately 180 days per year. Within schools, the curriculum and schedule continue to resemble that which was prevalent in the first half of the twentieth century. In fact, high school graduation requirements remain largely unchanged. Someone once said, "If Rip Van Winkle had gone to sleep January 1, 1900 and woke up on January 1, 2000, the only aspect of our society that would be familiar would be the school." That's probably correct. But if our schools are, as I believe, the most important institution in our society, it goes without saying that they must not only keep up with the changes in our society, but also anticipate the future. Our schools do none of that.

Failing to adjust to societal changes has caused our schools to educate poorly or to under-educate almost three generations of our citizens. The impact of this failure is readily seen in the children now coming into our schools. Poorly educated adults are more likely to live in poverty. Their lifetime income will be a third that of a college graduate. Children raised in poverty are the least prepared for learning. Today, most public school systems, particularly in urban areas, have a disproportionate number of children raised in poverty. In fact, researchers report that low-income students are now a majority in the public schools of the U.S. South, and that schools in the West may cross the line in the near future. Nationally, public schools average 51 percent of their students coming from families living in poverty.[11]

Harold Hodgkinson, an Alexandria, Virginia-based education demographer, states that the U.S. now has the highest percentage of children living in poverty of any of the twenty-four Organization for Economic Cooperation and Development member nations. The U.S. has held that distinction for more than ten years.[12]

In the above-cited 2015 report of the Southern Education Foundation, Vice President Steve Suitts quotes from the SEF's earlier report:

> No longer can we consider the problems and needs of low-income students simply a matter of fairness… Their success or failure, in the public schools, will determine the entire body of human capital and educational potential that the nation will possess in the future. Without improving the educational support that the nation provides its low income students—students with the largest needs and usually with the least support—the trends of the last decade will be prologue to a nation not at risk, but a nation in decline…"[13]

This is occurring even after the "War on Poverty" that was established in 1964 during the presidency of Lyndon Johnson. At that time, the country had 16 percent of its citizens living in poverty. Today, after more than $22 trillion[14] of expenditures to eliminate poverty, we have a poverty rate of 17 percent and growing. Though that is only a 1 percent increase, it adds up to 21 million more people due to the population growth of the nation. The War on Poverty has been an unmitigated failure because it is the wrong war. Poverty is not the lack of money; poverty is the lack of the ability to earn money. Had the Federal government spent a fraction of the money supporting the retraining of our adult workforce and helping to enhance our education system, we might very well have a different society today.

However, the government did not do that and we continue to turn out young people ill-prepared for the world in which they will live. This is a direct reflection of the failure of our public schools to adjust to both the changing demographics and to the significant societal and economic changes occurring. The net effect is that an increasing percentage of our children are not being effectively educated. Since this has been the case for decades, we have an ever-increasing percentage of under-educated adults.

Unless we improve our schools, we will continue to turn out young adults without the knowledge and skills needed to gain meaningful employment in an increasingly complex economy.

It is based upon that reality that this book is written. In the following pages, I will endeavor to provide a blueprint for the changes needed in our education system and the rationale for each. It is obvious that the country must effectively educate every child and it is equally obvious that we cannot do so with the present system of public education.

This book is divided into four sections. Part One deals with the existing arena of public education, Part Two delineates three specific deficiencies of the present system that must be addressed for meaningful change to occur, Part Three looks at some structural changes to enhance learning, and Part Four looks at some innovations that work and ends with a plan for change.

## Part One: The Current Landscape

THE FIRST four chapters look at the current state of our public education system.

Chapter 1, "The Existing System," describes our current schools. We will look at how schools are set up, how people enter the profession and how learning occurs or fails to occur in public schools.

Chapter 2, "External Factors," describes the external environment in which our public schools operate. This discussion is included because, over the last 70 years our entire society has changed, but our schools are still organized very much the same way. These societal changes have been labeled "External Factors." These factors have impacted our schools, but public school officials have almost no control over any of them. Failure of our schools to adjust to them has been very detrimental to our children. The list of such factors is quite extensive.

**Chapter 3, "The Mission of the School,"** discusses the what should be the goal of schools. This is a topic that everyone claims to understand yet when you dig into the subject, you find the reality is quite different. I found no one who could articulate a meaningful mission statement for schools, so I developed my own. Unless everyone agrees on the mission, it is impossible to create a system to achieve it.

**Chapter 4 "Union and Change,"** discusses teacher unions and change. In this chapter we look at how these unions developed, why they are so powerful, how they constrain change, and how they can be dealt with in our effort to improve schools.

## Part Two: Steps for Change

THE NEXT three chapters delineate three areas of reform that must be addressed before any other reforms can become sustainable. In this section we look at how teachers and education leaders are selected and trained. We also look at the governance structure and how it impacts our schools. All three chapters deal with the "people" issues of education.

**Chapter 5, "Teaching,"** deals with selection and training of teachers. Here we look at the profession that is the most important profession in our society, the one from which all others are born, and suggest how it needs to change to ensure a quality teacher in every classroom.

**Chapter 6, "Leadership,"** deals with the selection and training of educational leaders. If we improve teaching and do not improve leadership, we will fail. So, in this chapter we describe how leaders are now selected and trained and then describe how they should be selected and trained.

**Chapter 7, "Goverance,"** focuses on school governance. If we fix teaching and leadership but do not address governance, we will not succeed in fixing our schools. Ineffective governance is a roadblock to providing effective education for our children.

## Part Three: Next Steps

IN THIS section, we look at additional system changes that should be implemented once the first three are put in place.

Chapter 8, "Group versus Individualized Learning," looks at group versus individual education and suggests how we must change the system to meet the needs of the individual child.

Chapter 9, "A Longer Day/Year and Time Versus Achievement," discusses adopting a longer school day and school year along with the issue of time versus achievement. The current school calendar was established in 1904 and is still in use. Graduation requirements are based upon the accumulation of "credits." A credit represents 9900 minutes of seat time. It is not a measurement of learning. It's the wrong measurement.

Chapter 10, "Technology," focuses on how technology can be a "game changer" for education. Technology now allows children to learn 24/7. Also, technology can individualize education and needs to be effectively employed in the education of our children.

Chapter 11, "Choice, Vouchers, and Charters," discusses three major reform ideas: choice, vouchers, and charter schools. These three reforms are constantly mentioned in discussions on education. All three are good ideas, but they are not enough.

Chapter 12, "Brain Development and Childhood Education," takes a look at brain development and its impact on learning and then discusses early childhood education. Understanding how children learn and preparing children to learn is critical for success.

## Part Four: The Need and the Plan

IN THE last two chapters we look at practical steps that can be taken to improve our schools.

Chapter 13, "A Call to Action," demands action. Making our public schools work for every child is the most important thing we can do for our children and for our country. It is imperative that we deal with this institution now and make the changes needed to fundamentally improve the education provided to our children.

**Chapter 14, "The Game Plan,"** offers a specific plan at the state level. In this chapter, we endeavor to provide both a plan and the sequence of implementation. It is hoped that this plan, or something very close to it, will be adopted by at least one state in order to create a template for the nation.

Educating all our children will only occur if we fundamentally change our present system of public education. That can only happen with changes to state laws and codes. Some day, one state is going to take on this task. When that occurs, it will create a template for the transformation of our public school system. I hope this book might play some small role in making that a reality so that we, as a nation, can effectively educate *every child* in *every school.*

# ACKNOWLEDGEMENTS

FOR THE PAST 25 YEARS I HAVE BEEN ABLE TO SPEAK TO AND TO visit with many wonderful people (from business, government, and unions) on the subject of education—so many people that it would be impossible to include everyone. There were, however, some people who were particularly helpful and deserve special thanks.

This whole effort started in 1992 with a phone call to then-Secretary of Education, Lamar Alexander, now the current senior senator from Tennessee. I thank him for seeing me and introducing me to David Kearns, who was extraordinarily helpful. David was the former CEO of Xerox and was, when we met, the Deputy Secretary of Education. David started me on a wonderful path of learning.

One of my most meaningful encounters was with Betty Wallace, who was then the Superintendent of the Vance County School District in Vance County, N.C. She still is the most profoundly talented educator I have ever met.

Along the way, I was privileged to meet with leaders in all facets of government and education, including people like Ernie Boyer (President of the Carnegie Institute), Joel Klein (Chancellor of the New York Public Schools), Michelle Rhee (Chancellor for the District of Columbia Public Schools); Don Ingwerson (former Superintendent of the Jefferson County Schools, Louisville, KY), Dr. Martin Eaddy (Superintendent of Lincolnton, NC, School District); Arlene Ackerman (Superintendent of Philadelphia Schools); Barbara Byrd-Bennett (Superintendent of Cleveland, OH schools), Susan Enfield (Highline Schools in Washington State); John Fryer (Duvall County Public Schools in Florida); Richard DeLorenzo (Chugach School System in Anchorage, AK); Alan Bersin (San Diego); Tom Payzant (Boston); Diana Lam (Providence, RI); and Jerome "Jerry" Wartgow (Denver).

I also met with governors: the late Governor Booth Gardner (Washington), Bob McDonald (Virginia), Mitch Daniels (Indiana), Roy Romer (Colorado, and then-Superintendent of Los Angeles Schools), and James Hunt (North Carolina). Jeb Bush read the manuscript and provided helpful suggestions. Others who let me pick their brains on education issues included Rod Paige (Superintendent of Houston Public Schools and then Secretary of Education), Lou Gerstner (former Chairman of IBM and Chair of the Teaching Commission), Ross Perot (while working on education reform in Texas), John Doerr (Partner of Kleiner Perkins and The New Schools Venture Fund), Frank Schrontz and Phil Condit (both former Chairmen of Boeing), Christopher Cross (former Deputy Secretary of Education), and Terry Bergeson (former Superintendent of Public Instruction for Washington State).

School principals were helpful, particularly Marja Brandon, one of the finest educators I have ever known (Seattle Girls School), and Larry Rosenstock (creator of High Tech High in San Diego).

Union leaders also were helpful. I had the privilege of talking with and learning from Keith Geiger (NEA President), the late Al Shanker (AFT President), Carla Nuxol (President of the Washington State Education Association), the late Roger Erskine (Executive Director of the Seattle Education Association), and Dal Lawrence (former head of Toledo (Ohio) Federation of Teachers.

Deans of Education Schools and of Business Schools were of assistance. Those included Kim Clark (former Dean of the Harvard Business School), Bob Bruner (former Dean of the Darden School at the University of Virginia), Bob Pianta (Dean of the Curry School at the University of Virginia), Tom Stritikus and Pat Wasley (former Deans of the Education School at the University of Washington), Francisco Rios (former Dean of the Education School at the Western Washington University), Brian Burton (former Dean of the School of Business and Economics at Western Washington University), Kathleen McCartney (former Dean of the Harvard Graduate School of Education), and the late Sue Schmitt (former Dean of the School of Education at Seattle University).

I can't leave the higher education community without a special thank you to Professor Allen Grossman, chief developer of the Public Education Leadership Program (PELP) at the Harvard Business School, and to both Dean Robert Pianta and Dean Robert Bruner for their support in developing the dual degree program in education leadership at the University of Virginia. These three gentlemen are true leaders in improving the operational effectiveness of our country's schools.

Others in higher education include: Tony Wagner (Harvard Graduate School of Education), Stig Leschly (Harvard Business School), Tim Garson (former Provost of the University of Virginia), Dan Martin (President of Seattle Pacific University), Bruce Shepard (former President of Western Washington University), Father Stephen Sundborg (President of Seattle University), the late Elson Floyd (President of Washington State University), and Mark Emmert (former President of the University of Washington).

Special thanks go to the late John Stanford (former Superintendent of Seattle Public Schools), who taught me more about the power of leadership than anyone I have ever met, and to Joseph Oschefsky who followed John as Superintendent. I also want to thank several of my colleagues who served with me on the School Board of Seattle Public Schools: notably the late Ellen Roe, Linda Harris, Barbara Schaad-Lamphere, the late Al Sugiyama, Dr. Scott Barnhart, Nancy Waldman, Jan Kumasaka, Michael Preston, Barbara Petersen, and Steve Brown.

Others in the Seattle community who deserve thanks include: Artie Buerk (co-founder of the Alliance for Education), Robin Pasquarella and Sara Morris (both former Presidents of the Alliance for Education. Nearby, in Bellevue, Washington, were the late Mike Riley (former Superintendent of Bellevue Public Schools), and Judy Bushnell (former president of the Bellevue School Board), one of my mentors on so many education issues. I also want to thank Dr. John Medina, who is not only a friend, but was extremely helpful in providing me information for the commentary on brain development.

In the nonprofit world, I benefited from conversations with John Schnur (New Leaders for New Schools), Marc Tucker (president of the National Center for Education and the Economy), Eli Broad (Broad Foundation), Michael Feinberg (KIPP), and Liv Finne (Education Director of the Washington Policy Center). From the Gates Foundation, I appreciated my discussions with Tom Vander Ark and Vicki Phillips (both former heads of Gates Foundation education initiative), Martha Choe (former chief operating officer), and Bill Gates, Sr., who is not only a friend, but read the manuscript and provided some wonderful insights.

I especially want to thank Paul Guppy of the Washington Policy Center; my daughter-in-law, Sandy Nielsen; Kathy Henning of Seattle Pacific University; and Michael W. Perry of Inkling Books for their help in editing the manuscript. I also want to thank my daughter, Kristin Nielsen Merlo, for her assistance in editing this book. Kristin has become as passionate about education as have I, and I greatly value her views and her assistance.

Finally, I want to thank the staff of the Discovery Institute, including President Steve Buri, Chairman Bruce Chapman, Eric Garcia, Erik Nutley, Audrey Southgate, Bailey Takacs, and Anna Salick, for their wise counsel and support in making this book a reality.

# INTRODUCTION

SINCE THE EARLY 1990S, I HAVE DEVOTED A GREAT DEAL OF MY TIME to learning about and participating in the public educational system of our country. From that involvement, I have come to understand how the system works and have developed ideas on why it is failing so many of our children. I have concluded that the problem is not curriculum, or testing inadequacies, or our children's inability to learn. What I have concluded is that the issue is "system obsolescence." Our present education system is obsolete and no matter how we tweak it, it will never effectively educate all of our children.

> Our education system is stuck in time, training students for a world that no longer exists. Absent profound change to our schools, adults will keep piling up on life's sidelines, jeopardizing the survival of civil society. While not preordained, this is where America is headed.[1]

In this book, we will look at the present system and suggest why and how it should be changed. We will also point out that the change has to start at the state level with changes to existing laws and codes governing the operation of our public schools.

As a consequence, this book is primarily designed to assist state legislators and governors in helping them improve the education system of their state, but I also hope that parents and others interested in the education of our children will find value in its contents.

My experience and background is as a businessman and entrepreneur. I am not an educator and make no claims to be one. Rather, I am an interested and concerned citizen who has taken a serious look at our public education system.

In way of background, my wife Melissa and I were raised and educated in the State of Washington, attending public schools in Seattle. We both graduated from the University of Washington (1960 and 1961), after which we married and moved to Virginia, where I completed my six-month active duty tour with the U.S. Army. In 1961, we relocated to Boston where I attended the Harvard Business School, and she taught in a public high school.

After getting my MBA, we returned to Seattle, where I went to work for a large, Seattle-based company and my wife gave birth to the first of our three children.

In 1969, another fellow and I started a company in the basement of an A&P Store. In 1971, we purchased a Virginia-based company, Hazleton Laboratories, Inc.

For the next 23 years, while living in Virginia, we built that company into a multi-national business that was ultimately (1982) listed on the New York Stock Exchange under the name Hazleton Corporation. In 1987, we sold the company to Corning, Inc. I stayed on to run the company for another five years and retired in 1992.

At 54, I felt too young to fully retire. I had achieved my business goals and wanted to do something radically different with the rest of my life. I picked public education. That choice had many roots. First, I had served for many years on the board of Junior Achievement (JA) of Metropolitan Washington and served as chairman for three years. As part of my involvement with JA, I would periodically teach in local high schools. I was also a member of the Industrial Advisory Board of the Fairfax County Public Schools. (Fairfax County is a large county in Northern Virginia, just outside the boundary of the District of Columbia). There, I participated with other business leaders to assist the school system. One of our major accomplishments was the formation of the Thomas Jefferson School for Science and Technology. That school has gone on to be one of the best public high schools[2] in the country.

Personally, I had observed the education being provided to my three children in the public schools of Fairfax County. For one of them, the education was very good, but the other two tended to struggle and attended private school for their high school years.

As a businessman, I had observed the educational proficiency of people we hired, many of whom were unprepared for the work we needed performed. This included young people with not only a high school diploma, but also those with a certificate from a community college.

Finally, I observed the continuing decline of America's competitiveness in the world markets.

All these factors led me to take an interest in our public schools.

Since my wife and I wanted to return to Seattle, my involvement in public education became narrowed to "public education in Seattle." This led to the next question, "What are you going to do in public education in Seattle?" I did not know the answer to that question and so set out to do an intense study of the subject.

My first effort was to make a phone call to Lamar Alexander, then Secretary of Education and now the senior senator from Tennessee. At the time, my home was 20 minutes from his office. My phone call yielded a short meeting with the Secretary and an extensive meeting with the Deputy Secretary, David Kearns. David had been the CEO of Xerox Corporation prior to becoming Deputy Secretary. He and I met on three separate occasions, in 1992, to discuss public education. He also provided me with several names of people to whom I should speak. This began what became an odyssey into the world of education. Over the next two years, I talked with hundreds of educational leaders, including the heads of the two national teachers unions. I traveled to 19 states, met with five governors, visited scores of America's finest schools, both public and private, and met with the deans and faculty of two dozen education schools. I also read every book or report people recommended to me.

In my travels, I saw islands of excellence surrounded by a sea of mediocrity. I saw wonderful people doing amazing work, but in spite of the system, not because of it. Whenever I visited an outstanding school, I found an outstanding principal who acknowledged that he or she had to break some rules to achieve the goals they wanted. They would give teachers far more autonomy than was allowed, they would allocate resources differently than specified, often they used different curricula than mandated, etc. Nonetheless, they did it inside the system. Many of these schools would give any private school a run for their money. Such schools, many of which were in destitute neighborhoods with a large proportion of poor and minority children, were fountains of hope for their students. Learning was occurring in every classroom and there was an excitement in both the children and the teachers. But, I also saw a rigid bureaucratic system that resisted change.

As I delved further, I arrived at two conclusions. The first was the notion that to make a difference in public education you must get inside the system. I based this assumption on witnessing thousands, if not tens of thousands of people, who were doing their level best to help improve their schools, to no avail. I saw this all over the country and concluded that I had to get inside the system.

I quickly learned that I was not qualified to be a teacher (I was the president of a New York Stock Exchange company and had a Harvard MBA, but did not have a teaching certificate), nor was I qualified to be a principal (I had no principal certification). In 1993, no one would consider me as a candidate for superintendent. So, the only entry point available to someone like me was to run for the school board.

Next, I learned that most of the problems of our schools were in the urban systems where over half of our children go to school and where the vast majority of minorities attend school. So, I concluded I would run for the school board in an urban system. Since my wife and I wanted to live in Seattle, it was going to be the school board of the Seattle Public Schools.

With the decision to run for the school board, it was necessary for me to return to Seattle and establish residence so I could file for public office. However, my residence had to be in the district I was to represent. In Seattle, there are seven school board members and each one represents a district within the city. I decided that if I was going to win election, I had to run in a district where the incumbent did not seek re-election. This was important since I had been gone from the city for almost 23 years and no one knew my name or anything about me.

As fate would have it, the only incumbent who chose not to run in 1993 was the one who represented the district where both my wife and I had grown up and where we wanted to live again. Thus, we now live about a half-mile from my wife's childhood home.

In 1993, I ran and was elected to the Seattle School Board, where I served for eight years. At the time of my election, the school district had approximately 45,000 students and a budget of $297 million, with about 100 schools and 4,600 employees.

When I ran for the board, I had an agenda that I shared with my colleagues. This agenda had been developed from my travels. The first item on that agenda was to hire a new superintendent. The current superintendent was a wonderful man, but he was not a change agent. He had been superintendent for 11 years and the Seattle Public Schools had not materially improved under his leadership. I felt we needed a "change agent" if we were going to make major improvements.

It took a year for a majority of my colleagues to agree with me. Once we had the votes, it then became a question of the search. Washington State is one of only five states that do not require a superintendent to be certified. Thus, we were free to look outside education for our new leader. In fact, because I had traveled the country extensively looking for a district that had taken school reform to scale, I was able to absolutely assure my colleagues that the person we were looking for was not in public education. Had he or she been there, I would have found them.

To ensure we would see candidates from outside the field of public education, we selected a business search firm, as opposed to an education search firm. We told the firm to bring us a non-traditional leader. They found him in the form of retired Major General, John Stanford.

Stanford had been in the Army for 30 years, retiring as a Major General and then became the county executive of Fulton County, Georgia (the county which includes the city of Atlanta). During his tenure as county executive, Stanford had been able to move the county from the bottom third of counties in their financial ratings to the upper 10 percent. He had also funded over $1 billion of infrastructure for the county without raising taxes. In other words, here was a proven leader who had turned around a public system. Exactly the type of person we wanted.

John was hired and became superintendent in September of 1995. Though he only served two-and-a-half years (he died quickly after being diagnosed with acute leukemia), he helped orchestrate numerous changes that were implemented during his tenure and the three years following his death.

With the hiring of General Stanford, we were able to begin on the rest of the agenda. Below is a partial list of what we accomplished:

1. **Eliminated mandatory busing.** This was our first vote after John became superintendent. What we had learned was that 10 times more minorities were being bused than whites and that the academic achievement of those being bused was not appreciably higher than those not bused.

2. **Decentralized the system.** Too many decisions were being made at the district headquarters. We empowered our principals and gave them both authority and responsibility for how their school performed.

3. **Modified the union contract.** We were able to negotiate a change in the union contract that allowed principals to hire staff without regard to seniority. This was a big win and a necessary win because it was impossible to hold principals accountable if they had no authority over staffing.

4. **Changed how schools were funded.** When I was elected, the funding system used was called a *staffing standard*. That meant that the money budgeted to a school was based upon the number of adults assigned to that school. Adult assignment was based upon student population. Twenty-five students equaled one teacher. Five hundred students called for an assistant principal. This funding model made no sense and so we changed it to a *weighted student formula*. This model moved the money with the students and it took into account that certain students cost more to educate than do others. What this system yielded was more money for those schools that had the toughest students to teach. Just the reverse of what had been occurring.

5. **Adopted choice.** We recognized that parents, not the district, should be able to decide where their child attends school. In providing "choice," we gave a preference to the neighborhood school, but allowed parents to send their child to any school they wanted to, provided there was room and provided they could get their child to the building. If a child attended school outside their "catchment" area, there would be no transportation provided. (We subsequently modified our "choice" policy in order to provide limited transportation to those who could not transport their child to their desired school. We did this by providing transportation to four elementary schools, two middle schools and two high schools for all parents in the city. However, all schools were available without transportation.) This policy of providing choice put pressure on the schools to create a learning environment that parents wanted their child to have. It meant that schools had to attract parents or they would not be funded. It forced schools to do a self-analysis and create programs that attracted parents and children. Installing choice forced schools to improve.

6. **Established a Principal Training Institute.** Because we had dramatically changed the job of being a principal, it was necessary that we provide training to our principals to teach them how to budget and how to interview and hire staff—two tasks they had not been trained for and had never done.

7. **Passed levies.** Seattle schools normally tried to pass two levies every four years. One was an operating levy that was used to supplement state funding. The other was a capital levy that was used for new construction and major maintenance. Three prior capital levies had failed to pass. Shortly after Stanford's arrival, we put on the ballot a $339 million capital levy that passed. With that money, we were able to build or remodel 17 schools with the entire program coming in on time and on budget.

8. **Installed standards for every grade.** Neither the Board nor the Administration had a clear definition of what a child should know and be able to do at various stages of their school career. Thus, we decided we needed standards for each grade. This was an enormous task, but was completed after three years of effort.

9. **Reduced the dropout rate.** As schools improved, the dropout rate declined. This was a specific goal we had set for ourselves.

10. **Reduced truancy rates.** Truancy rates declined as the leadership and teaching in each building became more effective.

11. **Increased enrollment, after years of decline.** Since the early '70s, the enrollment in Seattle schools had been on the decline. When I attended Seattle schools, in the late '50s, there were over 100,000 children attending. By the late '80s, even though the city had grown in population, school enrollment had declined to under 40,000. During Stanford's Superintendency, enrollment not only increased, but families were moving back into the city to attend the public schools.

We made many more changes, but these were the major changes and, because of our progress, the Seattle schools were being recognized nationally as a district on the move.

I retired from the Board in 2001 along with two of my colleagues. Upon my retirement, the *Seattle Times* wrote an editorial (November 30, 2001):

> When Seattle School Board President Don Nielsen joined the board, the seasoned businessman made no bones about using this city as a template to transform education nationwide.
> He got part of the way.
> A look at the changes in the district during Nielsen's eight-year tenure as a leader and provocateur on the board is a reminder why, when he retires next month, his expertise will be missed.
> The district has come a long way toward being a quality system, and Nielsen deserves a large part of the credit.

Three of us left in 2001 and the other four members of the Board left in 2003. So, by 2003, Seattle Public Schools had an entirely new board who had entirely different ideas.

It has now been 18 years since I served on the Seattle School Board. In that time, with the exception of mandatory busing, virtually everything we put in place has been radically modified, terminated, or reversed. It's as if we were never there. New board members and new superintendents have come and gone and each have had their own agenda. The net effect is that Seattle's public schools, and the system under which they operate, are now very much like they were prior to 1993. What's even more painful to recognize is that this situation is not unique to Seattle. It happens in every city that has attempted massive change. Thus, the *status quo* is the only sustainable outcome.

Seeing all our work go for naught has caused me to change my thoughts on how we need to go about improving our schools. Initially, I thought one had to get inside the system to make a difference. I also thought the urban system was the entity of change. Basically, I have been proven wrong on both assumptions. Granted, getting inside the system will allow you to influence change, but it will not be sustainable. Also, it is obvious that the urban district is not the primary entity of change.

This has been a painful lesson, but a necessary one for me to really understand where the problems lie and what we need to do to solve them. What I have concluded is that *the entity of change is the state, not the district, not the school and not the federal government.* It is the state because the state controls most of the money, who can and cannot teach, who can and cannot lead, the governance model, the subjects taught, the rate of pay for staff, and the graduation requirements. As in any other organization, if you control the money and the people, then you control the operation. Thus, if we want to improve our schools, we must start with changing state laws and codes.

This book is written to give state leaders some background on the existing system, reasons why it is obsolete and to provide a template on what laws and codes need to change. Changing the system at the state level is the only way sustainable improvement can be made to our nation's schools. The book is also written to point out that more money is not the solution. Virtually nothing in this book will require increased funding in order to be implemented. However, the solutions will require political courage.

# PART ONE:
# THE CURRENT LANDSCAPE

# 1. The Existing System

In Figure 1 below, we observe that during the last 47 years, there has been an enormous increase in spending for the education of our children. However, during that period there has been no meaningful increase in the number of students in our schools. Spending has grown at ten times the rate of enrollment. Thus, we are now spending almost three times more per child, in inflation-adjusted dollars, to educate our children than in 1970. Most the money has gone to either increase the pay of educators or for an increase in the number of adults working in our public education system. We now have almost twice as many adults per student as in 1970. Growth in adult employment has grown four times faster than student enrollment.

In spite of these major increases in both money and staffing, there has been no appreciable improvement in the academic achievement of our children. This is shown in Figures 2 and 3 below.

One is forced, therefore, to conclude that improved academic achievement is not going to happen if we just continue to put more money into the system or hire more people to work on the issue. We've tried that and it hasn't worked!

As a student of our public education system, I have had the privilege of visiting schools in states all across the country. Some of these were America's finest schools. Students in those schools were receiving an excellent public education regardless of their race, ethnic origin, or socioeconomic status.

Visiting and observing these schools, I came to realize that public education can work. In our country, we have hundreds of wonderful public schools. In fact, almost every city has at least one, if not several, outstanding schools. Sadly, however, these schools are the exception, not

# Figure 1

## Trends in Spending, Staffing, and Enrollment since 1970

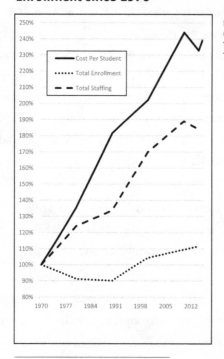

**Baseline 1970:**
Cost = $5,242 (2017 dollars)
Total Enrollment = 41,934,376
Total Staffing = 3,360,763

Source: National Center for Education Statistics
Digest of Education Statistics 2017
Expeditures: Table 236.70
Enrollment: Table 203.80
Staffing: Table 236.10

# Figure 2

## Average National Assessment of Educational Progress (NAEP) Reading Scale Score

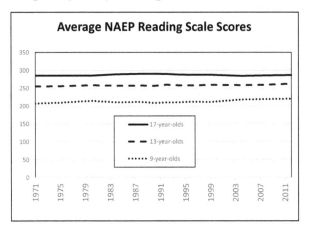

Source: National Center for Education Statistics
        Digest of Education Statistics 2017
        Table 221.85

# Figure 3

## Average National Assessment of Educational Progress (NAEP) Mathematics Scale Score

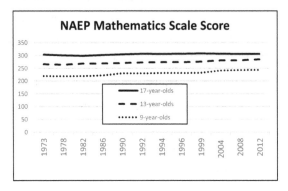

Source: National Center for Education Statistics
        Digest of Education Statistics 2017
        Table 222.85

the norm. The best of these schools have been thoroughly examined in various books, most of which now occupy space in my home library.

Seeing that the United States has wonderful schools, as part of the public system, I sought to find an entire school district that operated as effectively. I wanted to find a district in which all the schools, not just one or two, possessed the characteristics I had observed in high-performing schools.

After devoting nearly a year to the search, I found only one district that had endeavored to create an entire system that operated as effectively as the individual high-performing schools I had visited. That district was in Vance County, North Carolina, located about 60 miles north of Durham. The year was 1993. Then-Superintendent, Betty Wallace (she was subsequently fired), had transformed an entire district school system in three years, and the results were astounding. When Betty assumed leadership of the district, Vance County Schools were rated in the bottom 10 percent of all schools in North Carolina and were at risk of being taken over by the state. Betty came in, with a plan, and in three years Vance County Schools had improved so much the district was rated in the middle of all North Carolina school districts.

Vance County is a small rural area. At the time I visited this 7000-student district, about 60 percent of the students served were African-American, and about the same percentage of students lived in poverty. The area had two high schools, two middle schools, and ten elementary schools. Betty wrote about her experiences in Vance County and described her strategy for transforming public schools. Her book is called *The Poisoned Apple*, and I highly recommend it.

Visiting Vance County Schools, and talking at length with Betty Wallace, firmly convinced me that it is possible to transform an entire school district for the better. She did it, albeit on a small scale, and in doing so, she created a practical template that others could use.

Betty was fired a couple of years later, following her decision to terminate a school administrator. The administrator had been accused of sexual harassment. Betty's investigation of the charges gave her reason to believe they were valid, and she terminated the individual. Subsequently, the school board decided to side with the administrator and fired Betty for wrongful dismissal. Sadly, Vance County Schools were never the same.

Betty's ideas are as applicable today as they were when she implemented them back in the early 1990s. She knew that the problem of low-performing schools is not that the children can't learn; rather it is a function of the competency of the adults and the constraints of an obsolete system that hinders learning. She also knew that unless the system is dramatically modified, the effective education of all children is impossible. Betty worked on turning around a district, and she succeeded. After she left, however, the district soon went back to its old low-performance levels and, once again, began to fail the very children it was set up to serve. I experienced the same phenomenon in Seattle. Others have also seen the same thing occur—temporary success that is subsequently reversed. Sustainable change is virtually impossible to achieve in a school or a district.

Despite these setbacks, we must change the system because it is failing our children and our nation. Here is a review of the extent of the problem:

- Only 26 percent of high school graduates meet the college readiness benchmarks in all four subjects of the ACT Test (English, reading, mathematics and science).[1]
- Only 27 percent of fourth-graders and 32 percent of eighth-graders are proficient in reading, and fully 32 percent of fourth-graders and 22 percent of eighth-graders score "below basic."[2]
- Over 3 million students drop out of high school annually.[3]

- The U.S., which once had some of the highest graduation rates of any developed country, now ranks 22nd out of 27 developed countries.[4]
- The U.S. now ranks 27th of all developed nations in overall education proficiency of our students—just behind the Slovak Republic.[5]
- The U.S. spends 39 percent more per pupil than Germany, 33 percent more than France, and 39 percent more than Japan.[6]
- The United States has the largest per-capita prison population in the world, followed by Russia. The highest-scoring European countries in international education comparisons tend to be those with the lowest prison populations.[7]

Let's take a look at this system that is so badly in need of transformation.

Today's school system operates very much like a production line in an early twentieth-century factory. Every student, regardless of ability or preparation, attends school for the same length of time each day, each week and each year. Every student is taught the same curriculum, delivered in much the same way, and we expect the same outcome for nearly every child.

However, any person knowledgeable about production knows the only way a production line works well is if the incoming raw material is uniform in all respects. In education, we have anything but uniform raw material. Our students come from all backgrounds. They have different interests, different learning styles, different motivations, different levels of learning readiness, different home environments, different amounts of sleep the night before, etc. No two students are really alike, yet our present system treats them as virtually the same. *Our present system has never effectively educated every child, and it never will.* In fact, as mentioned earlier, the system was not designed to effectively educate every child, and it has successfully not done so for almost 120 years.

In repeated efforts to remedy this situation, Congress, state legislatures, and local school boards have all put in place thousands of regulations. Each of these regulations was designed to correct a perceived deficiency in the system. These regulations have been piled one upon the other to the extent that the system is now tightly handcuffed. Even the best principals and superintendents find it virtually impossible to operate an effective school or district under the current burden of rules, procedures and paperwork.

In fact, all of the effective schools in this country are excellent in spite of the larger system, not because of it. The leaders of these schools regularly break the rules or get waivers in order to educate their children. Frankly, it is the only way excellence can be achieved.

To substantiate the above points, let's look at the core structure of the current system.

## Teaching

To BECOME a teacher in any state, one needs to graduate from an approved college of education and gain *certification*. In most states, this is the only way to become an approved public school teacher. There are a few states with *alternative certification laws*, but these are narrow exceptions and only a small percentage of teachers gain entry into the education system through these alternative means.

The major exception is Teach For America (TFA). This organization hires young people who are some of the top graduates of their respective universities and provides an alternative certification process via training over a summer and then ongoing training during the first year of teaching. Teach For America currently has over 20,000 cohorts actively teaching in 38 states and the District of Columbia.[8] In addition, there has been some recent collaboration with other alternative certification programs and universities. One example is the Teacher Residency program now operating in several cities. This program, which primarily focuses on bringing in students of color, has provided an excellent program for enhancing the diversity of our teaching corps. Both of these programs still involve a very small number of teachers.

In most states, there are numerous institutions licensed to grant teaching certificates. In Virginia there are 50, and in my state, Washington, we have 25. Pennsylvania has over 90. As a nation, we have over 1400 such schools. The spectrum of quality between the best and the worst teaching institutions in each state is substantial. Moreover, there is no established standard to measure the effectiveness of any given educational training program. Again, there have been some recent moves to change this situation. Both North Carolina and Tennessee have moved to a *value-added measurement* of their education schools. That effort is gaining traction in other states as well.

Teachers gain their certification from their university upon graduation. Certification is a state-mandated requirement and must be met before a graduate can be hired by a public school district. Gaining certification, however, simply means one has completed the necessary course of study dictated by the state. It does not mean that a person has a proven ability to teach children. This is because most education schools do not have a required "proof of competency" in order to gain certification. As a consequence, *being "certified" is no guarantee of being "qualified."*

I do not mean to imply that we do not have competent teachers in our system. We most certainly do, and they are a gift to the students they serve. However, high-quality teaching is not the norm; it is the exception. This reality is caused by education colleges having very low standards of admission, mediocre course work and limited field training. Recently, a few states have recognized this issue and have installed what is called the *Teacher Performance Assessment* (TPA) or similar names. This is a relatively new effort and is being met by resistance from many education schools.

To graduate from a typical education school, the student must spend time teaching in a real classroom. It is called *student teaching*. These programs vary in length, but six weeks is not uncommon. A student may student-teach in a second-grade class, but upon graduation, that same student, who will now be certified in elementary education, may be hired to teach a fourth-grade class. This experience disconnect often happens and the effect is to put a new teacher into a classroom to work with students of an age she has never taught before, with a curriculum she has never seen before, in a school she has never visited.

Moreover, when a new teacher comes into a school, her students' previous teacher seldom provides any information about the class. To make matters worse, most districts do not supply the new teacher with meaningful lesson plans or details on how to teach the curriculum. That same new teacher will likely not be given a mentor, and more than likely will be assigned to the toughest classes in the lowest-performing schools. This is a recipe for failure.

In fact, thirty percent of teachers leave the profession within five years. In urban school systems, fifty percent leave within three years.[9] It is not hard to understand why.

Finally, data also tells us that the graduates who performed best in their college of education programs are the first students to leave the profession.[10]

As long as the most gifted education students leave the teaching profession early and as long as our brightest and most talented citizens are not entering the profession of teaching at all, we will not dramatically improve the quality of classroom instruction in our public schools. We will discuss this issue in more detail in Chapter 5.

# Leadership

EVERY ORGANIZATION needs effective leadership and in our school system, that leadership is provided by principals and superintendents.

## *Principal*

To become a principal also requires certification from an approved school of education. However, to gain admission for principal training, one must first have been a teacher for two or three years. In other words, one must have attended an education school, become certified to teach, and survived the first two to three years of teaching.

At most schools of education, there are no other qualifications needed to become a principal. One does not need to present recommendations from a principal or superintendent, nor have demonstrated leadership skills, nor have been an outstanding teacher. (In fact, some of our very worst teachers are the first ones to apply to become principals. If you can't make it in the classroom, become an administrator.) One merely needs to have taught for 2–3 years and have enough money to pay the tuition. Because many schools of education need students' tuition dollars, to apply is to be accepted; to be accepted is to graduate and to graduate, because of the demand for principals, is to get hired. In most states, a principal receives tenure in just three years, meaning public school students and teachers will have that person in a leadership position for 20 to 30 years. A few principal programs do have some selectivity, but they are rare and the selectivity is not extensive.

Principal certification is usually a one-year program and graduates receive either a master's degree in School Administration or simply a principal's certificate. Again, the only place you can get such a certificate is at an education school. As was the case with teacher training programs, the spectrum of quality between the best and worst principal training programs is substantial.

As a consequence of this system, what we have in education is *leadership by accident, not by design*. It is the only system in our society that I know of where *promotion is done by self-selection*. Nearly every teacher who seeks to become a tenured principal will become one, regardless of their lack of leadership and management skills.

## Superintendent

In most states, the principal self-selection process repeats itself at this level. Forty-five of the fifty states require that superintendents be certified and this is again obtained by attending an approved school of education. Most superintendent candidates receive a Ph.D. or a Doctorate in

Education, many with a major in curriculum studies. One can self-select into most of these programs just as easily as signing up for principal training.

Few schools of education have any meaningful leadership training programs and few recognize how different the job of superintendent is from other management positions, particularly in urban school systems. Superintendent candidates should receive training in organizational behavior, labor relations, finance and budgeting, technology, construction contracting, etc. Few, if any, such skills are taught in schools of education. Once again, public school districts end up with leadership by accident, not by design

Schools of education hold a monopoly on both the supply of teachers and of leaders for our schools. As will be detailed later, this single source of supply poses a major impediment to improving our schools.

We will talk more about education leadership in Chapter 6.

## Governance

SCHOOL DISTRICTS are governed by elected school boards. School board members are elected by the citizens of the community and generally serve four-year terms. School boards are set up to be policy-making bodies, but they regularly delve into operations. Though some candidates for school board are qualified to oversee the operation of a large and complex organization, the vast majority are not. This lack of competence often creates a leadership vacuum resulting in chaotic district governance.

The membership of school boards often changes as election cycles occur. Quite often, a majority of a board is changed in one election. When that happens, the policy direction of the district often changes. Sometimes, a board's new majority decides to hire a new superintendent. This regularly occurs in urban systems where the average tenure of a superintendent is only 3.6 years.[11] This high turnover of school board membership and of superintendents makes long-term improvement very difficult, if not impossible. Poor governance combined with ineffective leadership creates an impossible situation for the effective management of a school district. We discuss governance issues further in Chapter 7.

## Centralization

School districts are set up as centralized bureaucratic institutions. Virtually all decisions are made at the central office. Principals seldom have much authority over people, money, or curriculum, but they are expected to be accountable for how their school performs. Even a rookie student of management would recognize immediately that this arrangement is simply not reasonable. To effectively lead and manage any organization, the leader should have authority over hiring and a major portion of the budget. Few principals are granted such autonomy. Realistically, in most districts, principals control the opening of the school each day and ensuring that the school operates smoothly. Though they are held accountable for much more, that really is the limit of their authority. They are managers, not leaders.

Supposedly, principals are also to act as education leaders of their school. Some perform this function very well, but many do not. In either case, however, it is ludicrous to hold a principal accountable for the performance of the school's teaching staff when he/she has no say in the composition of that staff. As stated, decisions on staffing, budgets, and curriculum are generally made at the district level. This top-down situation, combined with the myriad of regulations imposed upon schools by both state and federal regulations, creates a system that perpetuates mediocrity and discourages innovation.

Joseph Olchefske, former superintendent of the Seattle Public Schools, describes America's education system as a "Soviet Union model" system. The former Soviet Union ran a national economy based upon a centralized system. In that system, large numbers of people were employed, but little work got done and those tasks that were performed were not done well.

This analogy, applied to our public school system, has considerable validity. A classic example of what I am talking about can be seen in the New York City Public School system. There, the school system employs more administrators than the entire nation of France and, at the state level, the State of New York education department has more education administrators than all the nations in Western Europe combined. Moreover, the New York City Public School system, with 1,000,000 students, has a central office staff of 6,000. The Archdiocese of New York, which operates hundreds of Catholic schools and serves over 200,000 students, has 35.[12]

## Time

OUR PUBLIC schools are a time-based system as opposed to an achievement-based system.

### *The School Day*

In almost all schools, the school day is six hours. The starting and stopping times vary between districts and between elementary and secondary schools, but the net amount of time, regardless of when the day starts, is six hours. In secondary school, the day is divided into periods of one hour (actually 50–55 minutes). In most schools, a period ends with the ringing of a bell, and then the students move to another class to attend another period. One period will cover one subject. Students may take English in first period, math in second period, history in third period, etc. In elementary school, the rigidity of this schedule is reduced as students normally have only one teacher and attend class in only one classroom. This situation tends to give elementary teachers more flexibility in terms of the time spent on a given subject in any given day. (This is not always the case, as some districts even specify the number of minutes an elementary teacher must spend on specific subjects.)

However, in secondary school, the day is generally fixed to a prescribed schedule of six periods. This situation forces teachers to develop lesson plans that will only take one period to deliver. The driver here is time, not learning. Teachers are forced to use the period to convey the lesson of the day. Some students may learn the lesson in 10 minutes; others may not understand it after 55 minutes. It doesn't matter. The period ends and the students have to leave to go to their next class.

Learning takes a back seat to time. The clock drives what occurs and, as a consequence, students soon learn that their learning and understanding is secondary to the teacher's need to cover the material. The control of the lesson by time affects a student's ability to achieve. If a student is a fast learner in English, but a slow learner in math, the present system will fail the student's learning in both subjects. Slow learners in math will quickly get turned off to the subject because they can't keep up. Ultimately, they will come out of high school under-educated in a core subject. Conversely, fast learners in math may be equally turned off because they get bored waiting for the class to progress.

## The School Year

The school year is 178–180 days in length, just slightly less than half a calendar year. The school year was originally set to comply with the student's need to help parents with farm labor and other tasks needed for the family to survive. In the early days of the twentieth century, this made sense. Young people didn't need a lot of education to survive, and there was always plenty of work to do at home. Today, however, that is no longer the case. Only three percent of America's families now work on the farm. Moreover, the educational needs of young people, including those who will become farmers, have grown exponentially during the twentieth century, but we still have the same school year. This school year means that our children are out of school 81 weekdays a year or about 16 school weeks: 365 − 104 (for weekends) − 180 (the school year) = 81.

Other industrialized nations have determined that a 180-day school year is insufficient. The education year for young people in other countries is quite different from what we provide to our children. From the longest to the shortest, the school year for other major nations is as follows:

Russia—210

Japan—200

Singapore—200

Germany—193

South Korea—190

England—190

Finland—187

Canada—183

USA—180[13]

*The United States has one of the shortest school years in the developed world.* Moreover, in many cases the school day is also longer in other countries. In Japan, for example, students go to school more hours per day, and more weeks per year than do American students. The net effect is that a Japanese child, upon graduation from high school, will have attended school for at least two American school years more than an American student in the same twelve-year period. In Singapore, they attend school one and a third years longer. It is little wonder that students in other countries are out-performing American students in international exams. In addition, some countries, like Finland, have extensive preschool programs designed to get all children well-prepared for learning prior to entering school.

## Grades

The class in which students are placed is also based upon time—only in this case it is really age. If a child is eight years old, that child is placed in the third grade. Not because that is their level of learning readiness, but rather because the child is eight. The child could be reading at the fifth-grade level, doing math at the fourth-grade level, and science at the second-grade level. However, because the child is eight, that child will take all subjects at the third-grade level regardless of how quickly or slowly they learn the material. All grades in our K–12 system are based upon age, not learning readiness or achievement levels.

*Graduation*

Graduation from school is also based on time. To graduate, after 12-13 years of school and receive a diploma, a student needs to collect a certain number of credits (called *Carnegie Units*). These units only apply to classes taken from the ninth grade through the twelfth grade. A credit is generally based on having received a passing grade for one year of class time or 9,900 minutes of instruction (55 minutes x 180 days). Half credits are sometimes given for a class lasting only a semester. A credit is not a measure of learning; it is a measure of time spent in class. Some refer to it as a "seat time" measure. In other words, to graduate from high school requires that a student spend a specific quantity of seat time in school attending specific classes.

Graduation occurs at the end of the twelfth grade, assuming the student has a sufficient number of credits. Up to 24 credits can be required for graduation. Normally, a student needs to earn four credits in English, three in math, three in science, etc. In fact, students not only need to acquire a certain number of credits to graduate, they need them in the proper subjects. I once witnessed a situation in which a student did not graduate because he lacked a half-credit in physical education (PE).

What all of this says is that seat time, rather than real learning, is the primary measurement used for meeting graduation requirements. Expressed another way, in public education, measuring input is more important than measuring output.

## Group versus Individual

I HAVE described our system of education as a *factory model*. Every child in a class is taught to the same curriculum, delivered the same way for the same length of time each day. However, every child is different. Students arrive at school with widely differing levels of learning readiness. Some pick up reading quickly, others find it very difficult; some find math interesting, others do not, etc. In our system, the student's particular interests and aptitudes are really irrelevant. The group receives the instruction and if some students understand the material and some do not, that is considered okay. I classify this as a system focused on teaching rather than on learning.

> In the typical American classroom, students are told what to study and when to study it. They cover content, rather than develop anything essential. They're pushed to jump through hoops and outperform peers, hollowing out any sense of purpose. Even top academic achievers retain little from their coursework.
>
> Today, the purpose of U.S. education is to rank human potential, not develop it.[14]

Again, not every school works this way and certainly not every classroom, but as a total system, this description is accurate.

## School Funding

Not only do principals seldom have control over the money spent within their school building; most states fund their public schools in a one-size-fits-all manner. This funding is generally based on the number of students enrolled in the school system. Some states provide a slight increase in funding for a non-English speaking child and both the states and the federal government provide additional money for special education children. These funding variances tend to help, but tend not to cover the additional costs necessary to provide the needed services to these special needs children.

For example, a child who speaks no English and is entering kindergarten is a relatively easy problem to overcome. However, a student entering high school who does not speak English is another story altogether. In most state-funding patterns, those two children would be funded for the same amount. The same is true for special education children, although there are four levels of funding for these children. A child who has slight dyslexia is one issue; a child who is a paraplegic or a child who is deaf or developmentally disabled is entirely different. Though funding patterns differentiate severely handicapped children from those who are modestly handicapped, the amount of money allocated for the former is nowhere near sufficient for the educational costs incurred. The law requires that these children receive as normal an education as possible, as well they should, but the amount of money provided is insufficient to comply with the law. The net effect is that money is diverted from regular students to help fund the needs of special education students.

In some states, local property taxes constitute the primary source of funding. In these states, there is also inequitable funding as property-rich communities can better fund their schools than property poor districts. Funding per student can vary by thousands of dollars per year in these states.

States also set compensation and benefit levels for teachers. Salaries for teachers tend to be based upon years of service and credits or advanced degrees attained. Virtually no compensation is tied to real classroom performance, or to the proven ability of a teacher to advance the learning of children under his or her care.

## Conclusion

FROM THE description above, it is easy to understand why so many of our children do not receive the education they need and deserve. The system is the problem. Unless and until we change it, we will constantly be disappointed by our inability to improve the level of student achievement.

Over the past fifty years, policy-makers have initiated dozens of education reform programs that were supposed to improve student achievement. Many had some positive effect, although some were detrimental. Most did little more than tweak the system, rather than change it. Really good ideas employed in a flawed system will rarely have any meaningful impact. That certainly has been the case with public education. All of the reform ideas of the past four decades have had little, if any, positive impact on student achievement. Also, we have witnessed that investing more money into a failed system will simply produce a more expensive failed system.

To summarize five core aspects of our public education system, what we have is:

1. An adult-focused system, but we need a student-focused system.

2. A teaching-focused system, but we need a learning-focused system.

3. A group-based system, but we need an individual-based system.

4. An input-focused system, but we need an output-focused system.

5. A time-based system, but we need an achievement-based system.

In other words, our present system is wrong and no matter how much we attempt to improve it, it will never meet the needs of all our children or of our society. To make real progress we must fundamentally transform the public education system.

Changing the system to operate differently in the above five areas will, over time, result in enhanced learning for all of our children.

It is my belief that the most important institution in our free democratic society is our public school system. Fixing our schools, so they work for all students, is not only the right thing to do for our children, it is the right thing to do for our country.

If we are serious about educating all our children, we must first fundamentally change the existing system of public education. The change must start with state laws.

# 2. External Factors

OUR PRESENT SYSTEM OF PUBLIC EDUCATION IS OBSOLETE. THAT IS true not only because the school system was designed as a production line to meet the needs of an earlier historical era, but also because it was designed for an earlier social era. The historical setting was important, but sweeping societal changes have, over the past hundred and fifty years, played a major role in making today's education system even more obsolete. These societal changes are seldom mentioned in the current debate about how best to improve education. Nonetheless, they have greatly influenced our schools, though school administrators had little or no control over any of them. Thus, they are labeled *external factors*.

In this chapter we will briefly review the major external factors that have had a material impact on our schools' ability to educate our children. The factors below are listed not in order of importance, but rather chronologically. The societal changes require us to rethink how we go about educating our children.

## World War II

IN THE decades prior to World War II, our public school system operated pretty well. The school system, as it developed in the late 1800s, provided our country with the educated workers it needed. For almost sixty years, the system worked as designed and the country prospered. Manual labor was the predominant type of work, and the level of learning provided was sufficient.

World War II created an increased need for factory workers, engineers, and other technically trained individuals. At the same time, women entered the workforce in unprecedented numbers.

The GI Bill, enacted after the war, created the opportunity for millions of young men and women, often the first in their families, to go to college. The result was an enormous increase in the number of our citizens who had advanced education. This, in turn, created a significant increase in our productive economy and in our exports of goods and services. Incomes rose, not only because of the increased quality of our workforce, but because many women were now making very good wages and salaries, thereby raising the income and standard of living for their families.

The middle class grew dramatically during this period. Housing became a boom industry as cities expanded and suburbs began to be formed. Also, the size of houses increased dramatically. Cars became affordable for most households and we saw the beginning of the two-car garage and the two-car family. Day care was another growing industry, and many children now spent much of the day with non-family members.

With prosperity came an increasing number of divorces. As the economy came out of the Depression, the unemployment rate declined and the divorce rates increased. In the early part of the twentieth century, divorce affected less than 10 percent of marriages.[1] During the Depression, the rate approached 20 percent. By the end of WWII, it had increased to 27 percent and by the mid-1980s, half of all marriages ended in divorce.[2] The impact of a marriage breakup on children is substantial. Increasing numbers of children came to school from single-parent homes. These single parents had less time to spend with their children and even less time to spend at their children's school. Parental involvement in children's education declined. The net effect was more pressure on schools to provide much of the non-academic development work in raising a child that had formerly been provided in the home.

## Women in the Work Force

BEFORE WORLD WAR II, women were employed outside the home primarily as teachers, nurses, and secretaries. A few were stewardesses.

The fact that women were restricted to a narrow range of professional career options meant that teaching attracted a disproportionately large number of well-educated and talented women from relatively high-status backgrounds.[3]

As opportunities for women expanded and more women entered other professions, the number, and in many cases the quality, of women entering the teaching profession declined. According to Sedlak and Schlossman, "Those who defected were mainly wealthier, smarter and more often married than those who continued to teach."[4]

Though many talented women continued to become teachers, many of the best and brightest were able to find employment in other fields. While this occurred, the post-war baby boom caused a rapid expansion in the number of students attending school and an expansion of the number of schools and classrooms throughout the country. The result was more children in school, but fewer top-quality teachers to educate them.

## The Interstate Highway System

IN 1956, President Eisenhower and Congress passed the Federal Aid Highway Act. This legislation called for the creation of an interstate highway system, and began the process of building four-lane, all-weather, divided highways across the country and through virtually every major city.

These new high-speed road systems served to expand the metropolitan area of all our major cities. Middle-class families continued their migration out of our cities to the suburbs, where they could get a bigger house and yard for less money and still be a reasonably short (time-wise) drive from work. The mass exodus from our cities served to decrease the size of urban school systems and to reduce the number of middle and upper-class children who attended those schools. The families who remained, tended to be those who could not afford to move—that is, families living in poverty and newly arrived immigrants.

Urban school districts experienced a decline in revenue as their tax base diminished and enrollment declined. Simultaneously, they experienced an increase in the percentage of students of color, of students whose primary language was not English, and of students being raised in poverty or in very poor economic conditions. These students, for the most part, were coming into school with far less preparation for learning than students whose parents had moved the family to the suburbs. Though the remaining students were perfectly capable of learning, they were less prepared for academic work. Poorly prepared students take more time and effort to educate. Thus, the cost of educating each student was higher than for those who had left the urban school system. This increase in the cost to educate each student, combined with reduced tax revenues, resulted in a dramatic decline in the quality of education available to students in urban centers. It also caused urban decay in many cites.

## The Civil Rights Act and Mandatory Busing

WITH PASSAGE of the Civil Rights Act in 1964, school districts that were operating racially segregated schools were required to integrate their schools. The courts and school administrators chose mandatory busing as the policy for accomplishing this. There is no question that ending school segregation and other forms of racial discrimination was the right thing to do. Desegregation was long overdue. However, the way our country implemented the new law often had a profoundly negative impact on the quality of our public schools and on the students the Civil Rights Act was designed to help.

Prior to the implementation of the Act, most African-Americans (particularly in the South) attended segregated schools. These schools were publicly funded, but were not funded to the same level as white schools. Thus, African-American children attended schools where the buildings were not as new or nice as the white children's schools and where the resources available to the children were substantially less. The conditions of schools in Virginia were indicative of schools in many southern states:

Very few black Virginians received any education at all until public schools were established during Reconstruction. Public schools in Virginia were segregated from the outset, apparently without much thought or debate, on the widely held assumption that such an arrangement would reduce conflict. Of course, public schools were segregated in many other states, both North and South.

Black schools, therefore, received far less financial support than did white schools. Black schools had fewer books, worse buildings, and less well-paid teachers. Ramshackle, segregated schools marked black Virginians with a stigma of inferiority and the status of second-class citizenship that they would have to endure throughout their lives.[5]

As the Act started to be implemented, African-American children would attend an all-white school where their teacher was also certain to be white. Moreover, that teacher likely had never taught an African-American child.

To make matters worse, the law required that schools be integrated throughout a given city, which meant that both white and black students would be removed from their immediate neighborhood and bused to other schools. Parents who had bought homes, based upon their assessment of the nearby schools, were now reconsidering. Some parents chose to comply with the busing requirements, but many (who could afford to do so) refused and took their children out of the urban public school system. These parents either moved to the suburbs or placed their children in private schools. Either decision had a further negative revenue and cost impact on urban public school systems.

The combination of better highways, being able to buy more house for the same or less money, and the imposition of mandatory busing had the effect of emptying major cities of middle- and upper-class families and the taxes they provided. The schools were severely impacted. Urban school systems were left with the most difficult-to-educate children (those living in poverty and those whose primary language was not English) and a decreasing tax base to pay for it. The effect was urban decay and we are still suffering from it. For example, today the city of Chicago has a public school system made up of 86 percent children of color and 87 percent children living in poverty.[6]

Many people believe the middle- and upper-class flight from the cities was due to racism. No doubt racism played a role. However, I believe the bigger reason was the failure of government officials to understand who is responsible for a child's education. Most educated parents, of whatever color, recognize that one of their primary responsibilities as parents is to secure a good education for their children. One of the ways parents do that is by picking the school their children will attend. For many families, this is done by choosing the neighborhood in which to live.

When the courts or the school district officials imposed mandatory busing, they took that school selection decision away from parents. *The lesson here is clear. Governments and school officials need to understand that the primary responsibility for the education of a child rests with that child's parents, not the school, not the district, not the state or federal government. Politicians should be very careful about making rules or laws that infringe on that responsibility.*

## The War on Poverty

Also in 1964, Congress launched the so-called "War on Poverty." At the time, sixteen percent of Americans lived below the government measure of poverty. The country's population was approximately 192 million. Thus, almost 33 million people lived in poverty.[7] How successful was this war on poverty? Michael Turner writes:

> In 2012, the federal government spent $668 billion to fund 126 separate anti-poverty programs. State and local governments kicked in another $284 billion, bringing total anti-poverty spending to nearly $1 trillion. That amounts to $20,610 for every poor person in America, or $61,830 per poor family of three.
>
> Spending on the major anti-poverty programs increased in 2013, pushing the total even higher.

Over the last 50 years, the government spent more than $16 trillion to fight poverty.

Yet today, 15 percent of Americans still live in poverty. Nearly 22 percent of children live in poverty today. In 1964, it was 23 percent.[8]

The U.S. Census Bureau figures bring us still closer to the present day: In 2016, there were 40.6 million people living in poverty.[9]

Thus, after spending more than $16 trillion dollars on the War on Poverty, we now have seven million more people living in poverty then when the war began over 50 years ago.

In other words, the War on Poverty has been an unmitigated failure. It failed, not because it was not a good cause, but because the programs created under it were waging the wrong war. There is no question that persistent poverty was and is a major problem facing our nation. In the 1960s, the government defined the problem correctly, but did not define the source of the problem correctly. To correct poverty, our country established our welfare system and, over time, failed to end poverty while creating millions of welfare-dependent families.

Poverty is defined as having a lack of money, but the cause of poverty is not a lack of money itself, it is the lack of an ability to earn money. If, instead of spending $16 trillion on "anti-poverty" programs, the government had spent a fraction of that amount of money on improving the effectiveness of our worker-training programs, and if we had improved our schools, we would have substantially reduced the poverty rate in this country.

The failure of the War on Poverty has affected our schools in a material way. Numerous studies by the U.S. Department of Education have shown that children raised in poverty are the least-prepared children any school receives. These children lack the resources available to other children. These children seldom have been exposed to books at home, have often not been read to by their parent or parents, and have lived in an environment where learning was not promoted or stressed. In many cases, the home environment may actually be detrimental to the child's education. Moreover, these children will not have had the life experiences that middle- and upper-income parents provide for their children.

Schools with high numbers of children, from families living in poverty, face greater educational challenges than schools composed mostly of middle and upper-class students. Urban school systems, because of the conditions mentioned earlier, have a disproportionate number of these hard-to-teach students.

## The Rise of Teachers Unions

UP UNTIL the 1970s, most teachers were not required to join a union as a condition of their employment. In fact, until 1969, the National Education Association (NEA), the nation's largest teachers' union, was a professional association operated by school administrators. Until then, decisions regarding how schools would operate were made by administrators and elected school board members.[10]

Between 1960 and 1977, union membership grew from virtually zero to almost 70 percent of all teachers.[11] This was caused by the passage of laws that allowed for government employees to be unionized. The National Labor Relations Act (NLRA) of 1935 began the rapid growth of unions in the private sector and by the late 1950s, organizing of government workers had begun. Further developments are described by Terry Moe:

> When it comes to teachers, for instance, only one state had a labor law in 1955 authorizing collective bargaining, but by 1980, some thirty states had adopted such laws.[12]
>
> California, for example, adopted its collective bargaining law in 1975 and a portion of teachers covered by collective bargaining jumped from just 8 percent in 1975 to 51 percent in 1976 and 85 percent in 1977. In Michigan, the new law was adopted in 1965 and bargaining coverage soared from 18 percent in 1964 to 85 percent in 1966. Minnesota adopted its law in 1971 and coverage grew from 3 percent in 1970 to 47 percent in 1972 and 94 percent in 1975.[13]

Today, the NEA has a total membership of 3.2 million and has become the most powerful union and political force in the country. The union is now a major force in dictating how local public schools operate and what management practices are and are not allowed in schools. We will further discuss the influential role of unions in Chapter 4.

## The Global Economy

IN THE late 1970s and early 1980s, America was losing its competitive advantage in the global marketplace. As transportation costs declined, foreign-produced goods were able to enter our markets at prices below domestically produced goods. Japan was becoming a powerhouse economically, and other Asian nations were developing extensive manufacturing capabilities. In addition, the quality of products made overseas was, in many cases, even better than those produced here. The net effect was a massive decline in the quantity of American manufacturing, as more and more foreign goods entered our markets and our own manufacturing companies moved production offshore in order to remain competitive. As companies moved production off-shore, urban centers saw a major decline in middle-class jobs. Urban centers were particularly hard-hit by this trend, and their schools again lost the children of middle-class families.

While this trend was occurring, a modern service economy was developing. The vast majority of jobs in this sector were low-paying, unskilled positions. People living in poverty or near-poverty, and recently arriving immigrants, filled jobs in the service sector. The growth of this sector fueled an increase in immigration, particularly of Hispanic and Southeast Asian families. These new arrivals were largely uneducated or under-educated adults. Upon arrival, their children were enrolled in our public schools, particularly in urban centers. The service sector of the economy continued to grow as we entered the Information Age.

## The Information Age

As COMPUTERS came into use and the Information Age was born, we saw an increasing need for our young people to be trained in science and math. Demand for workers with these skills increased dramatically, as did the compensation offered for this type of work. This further exacerbated the gulf between people working in low-paying jobs in the service sector (or living on welfare) and skilled workers making increasing amounts of money in the information sector. As jobs in this high-tech industry grew and became increasingly important, the gap between the haves and have-nots expanded again.

In our schools, money was being spent on technology and science. However, it was largely in the suburbs, as most urban systems were housed in old buildings with antiquated electrical systems and little money available to rewire buildings and/or acquire technology. Students attending urban schools fell further and further behind. Even in urban schools, where new technology was put in place, many of the teachers were ill equipped to utilize it effectively. We'll discuss this issue further in Chapter 10.

## Immigration Policies

BEFORE WWII, people could immigrate to the United States provided the paperwork was complete, certain requirements were met, and the immigrant quota the U.S. had set for their home country was not filled.

That policy affected my own family. In 1927, my father, who was born in Denmark, wanted to come to the United States to learn English. He found he could not enter the U.S. that year because the quota for Danes was filled. The next country he chose, Canada, had similar policies to those in the U.S., and, although the quota for Danes had not yet been reached, Canada would not let him enter without a sponsor and a job. He was able to secure both, and immigrated to Manitoba, where he worked on a farm owned by a Danish immigrant. After WWII my family immigrated to the U.S.

The story of my father is not unique to that era. Immigration laws were stringent and entry quotas were set for nearly every country. Most immigrants, prior to 1950 were from Europe with a lessor number from Asia.

Over the last seventy years, America's immigration policy has changed dramatically. Beginning with the Korean War and continuing since, this country has opened its borders. Refugees from Korea and Vietnam were welcomed after those wars ended. In the last 40–50 years, millions of immigrants have come into the U.S. by simply walking in, by being picked up in boats and by receiving transportation assistance from family members already here. These immigrants came mostly from Latin America and Asia. Countries such as Vietnam, Cambodia, Korea, the Philippines, the Pacific Islands, Mexico, Honduras, and Brazil were all sources of new immigrants to this country.

In almost every case, these immigrants were the poor of their countries and few had been provided any meaningful level of education. Most could not read or write in their native language, let alone in English.

These immigrants arrived and began to fill jobs in the service economy. By finding positions as maids, janitors, gardeners, farm workers, etc., these hard-working adults could earn a living without learning to speak English. Though most of these immigrants found jobs, they did not earn incomes that lifted them out of poverty. As a consequence, the children of these new families entered our schools not speaking English well and not well-prepared to learn. In states such as Florida, Texas, Arizona and California, Hispanic children are now the dominant population in some public schools, and they make up more than half of the students in some school districts.

We now have schools in major cities where the student population is 100 percent minority children and where 80 to 90 percent of those children qualify for free or reduced lunches (one of the federal government's measures of poverty). Schools, with these demographics, face a very difficult challenge. Not only are the children likely to be behind in their learning; they also may not speak English. When I was on the school board in Seattle, we had over 70 different languages spoken by children in our schools.

## African-American Population Growth

WHILE THESE momentous events were taking place, the U.S. African-American population continued to grow. Today, America is home to an estimated 43 million African Americans. These citizens have suffered from racism and discrimination for centuries, and, though equality is now the law of the land, racism's tragic legacy still affects our society and our schools.

Prior to 1867, few blacks had an opportunity to receive a good education and in some states it was illegal to teach a slave to read. For the next 80 years, most black children were educated in segregated schools. (Some black schools were excellent, but most were underfunded and under-resourced.) With the passage of the Civil Rights Act, African-Americans gained access to integrated schools, but in most cases they still did not receive the same education as white students. Many teachers tended to treat them differently by having lower expectations, and the overall system did not understand the African-American culture.

A large percentage of African Americans were born out of wedlock and were raised by a single parent. That trend has continued, and today 72.2 percent of African-American children are born out of wedlock.[14] Often, that single parent is also employed outside the home, which further reduces the time spent with the children. This situation further inhibits the learning readiness of these children, which increases their educational needs when they arrive at school.

Like the Hispanics and Asians mentioned earlier, African-American families predominantly live in urban settings. We are now nearing the end of the third generation of African-Americans who have had full access to a public school education. Though progress had been made, there still exists a major gap between the educational attainment of African-Americans and both whites and Asians.

Hispanics are now the largest minority group, surpassing African Americans, and they have a similar social profile regarding both out-of-wedlock birth rate (53 percent)[15] and the number of children raised in poverty. Hispanic families often struggle with the added problem of not speaking English.

## Individuals with Disabilities Education Act (IDEA)

OVER THE years, Congress has enacted numerous laws that have impacted schools. In fact, for most public school systems, the federal government accounts for about 50 percent of the regulations governing the operation of schools, yet it provides less than 10 percent of the funding. At one time, I suggested to my colleagues on the Seattle School Board that we consider not accepting any federal money so we could rid ourselves of all these regulations. My colleagues did not agree with that idea, but I was, and still am, convinced that federal regulations cost local school districts an amount much more than they receive in funding.

Of all the acts passed by Congress, the most onerous for schools is the Individuals with Disabilities Education Act (IDEA). This law requires public schools to provide an education to children with disabilities. One cannot argue with the goal of the law. The problem is with the lack of funding provided and the regulations covering these children.

Children with disabilities deserve the best education we can provide, just as all children do. However, we need to recognize that children with disabilities present new and difficult problems, both to the classroom teacher and to the school and school district.

Children who are blind, deaf, or disabled physically or mentally add another dimension to the task of educating all children. In some cases, a child with disabilities will require a one-on-one, full-time teacher. Such children typically cost a school district between $50,000 and $80,000 a year, yet most districts are given only a fraction of that amount for the education of that child. Even so, the district is required by law to provide for the child's education. As a result, school districts must allocate money from regular students to fund the educational needs of their students with disabilities. Also, the law does not take into account the difference in cost between educating a mentally disabled child and of educating a physically disabled child. The latter may add some expense in a classroom, but the former can be very disruptive to a classroom.

Handicapped students, particularly those with mental disabilities, require instruction from a very specialized and gifted teacher. Teachers like these are in short supply, so teachers who have received little or no training in special education often end up trying to teach these children. This situation is unfair to the teachers, to the child and the child's parents, and to the other children in the classroom.

The need to educate disabled children tends to occur mostly in urban school systems, where administrators are least able to cover the extra costs involved. Urban school systems face this dilemma because most hospitals are located in large cities. Parents with disabled children often position their family's home near these medical centers and enroll their children in the local school system.

## Technology

PERHAPS NO change in our society has affected learning more than the advent of computer technology. Today, young people have the world at their fingertips and they potentially can be learning 24 hours a day, 7 days a week. Most of us, who are middle-aged or older, find we need a younger person's help when we have a technical problem with our computer, cell phone, or other electronic devices. Today's young people are growing up in a technological world, but our schools have not kept pace. Technology, in my opinion, is the greatest improvement in individualizing education since the one-room schoolhouse. Neither the infrastructure of our schools nor the competency of our teaching corps is keeping pace with this new phenomenon. Technology has the potential to revolutionize learning and redefine the meaning of school—in fact, has already done so in many schools. We'll discuss this issue more in Chapter 10.

# Culture

THOUGH WE seldom talk about it, culture plays a big role in the academic achievement of children and is something over which schools have no control. For example, we see that Asian children routinely perform at high academic levels while African-American and Hispanic children often perform at low levels. Much of this difference arises out of the differing cultures of these student populations. Asians, particularly ethnic Chinese, Japanese, and Koreans, have a culture based on close family ties where education is stressed from the moment a child is born. Adult family members work hard to ensure the successful education of their children. This seems to occur regardless of the education level attained by the adult members of the family.

This focus on education manifests itself in the performance of Asian children who consistently outperform other demographics, including whites. Part of this difference can be attributed to the high level of poverty and single-parent households, but one must also acknowledge that culture plays a big role in the different outcomes.

The impact of family culture is immediate and begins at birth. Children raised in a typical high-poverty home (often a single-parent minority household) are exposed to less than one-third the number of words that are heard or read in a home where both parents are white and have earned a college degree. Similarly, children in these two types of homes are exposed to totally different learning experiences, with the latter having a much broader knowledge base on which to draw by the time they enter kindergarten.

Also, throughout our society, the increase in the number of families with both parents working is having an impact on our culture. In 1996, a study done by Laurence Steinberg of Temple University, showed that one in three parents are totally disengaged from the life of their adolescent child, especially the child's education.[16] Though the data from 1996 is not recent, there is no new evidence to suggest this cultural situation has improved.

According to Steinberg, "Widespread parental disengagement has left a large proportion of adolescents far more susceptible to the influence of their friends than in past generations, and this influence is taking its toll on school achievement."[17] Later in the study, Steinberg concludes: "No curriculum overhaul, no instructional innovation, no change in school organization, no toughening of standards, no rethinking of teacher training or compensation will succeed if students do not come to school interested in, and committed to, learning."[18]

As the population of the country has become more diverse, the impact of culture plays an increasingly important role in the ability of public schools to educate all of our children. In the near term, public schools will have little, if any, opportunity to influence the culture significantly. Over time, however, if our schools effectively educate every child, the cultural differences among races and ethnic groups will diminish as a more unified American culture is reestablished.

## Conclusion

ALL THESE external factors have materially affected our public schools, particularly schools located in urban centers. Today, we are pressing for better performance from our schools. We are installing new standards for learning and demanding more accountability from our educators. Given these trends, we need to recognize that at the very time when we want and need the most highly educated workforce in our history, we are dealing with the most difficult-to-educate population of children this country has ever seen.

We naturally tend to compare today's schools with those of yesteryear, but that approach is flawed. Today we have many more regulations than in the past. Unions are strong at all levels of the education system and have negotiated strong constraints on management. We have far more children who don't speak English as a first language. We have many more children being raised in poverty and/or in single-parent families. We have more children living in homes where education is not stressed. And, we have more special needs children to educate, a task for which our schools were not designed and for which most of our educational staff have not been trained. Finally, we are asking our schools to provide many services to students that formerly were provided at home. All this is occurring when our society and our economy need to have children learn at higher levels than ever before. Taken together, this presents us with a daunting challenge.

In spite of all these trends, I believe the public education system can be made to work, because I have seen it work in individual schools and it is working in several other countries. In the rest of this book, I will lay out the policy changes I believe are necessary to make the system work for all children. I will also suggest that unless and until the system is changed, we should not put large amounts of new money into the existing, outdated and obsolete system. What is needed is a new system.

# 3. The Mission of School

THE MISSION OF SCHOOL MAY SEEM SIMPLE. HOWEVER, I FOUND very little agreement on what is the mission of school. In fact, I would argue that this lack of a common understanding is one of the major reasons schools and school districts fail to effectively educate such a large percentage of their students. The development and solid support of a mission statement is, in my opinion, essential to improving the educational attainment of students served by our public schools.

As I traveled around the country, I asked hundreds of people involved in education the simple question, "What is the mission of school?" I asked because I was genuinely interested in knowing what we were trying to do with school. I had never thought about that question before, but I assumed people in the world of public education would definitely know. They would be able to tell me and I could then get on to the question of how best to help schools achieve their mission.

Perhaps not surprisingly, I found there was no common definition or firm knowledge about the mission of school. Everyone had an opinion, but none was very specific nor of much help in providing clear direction for managing a school.

Many times I asked the question and received a blank stare. Sometimes I received an amused look. In some cases I was looked upon as being stupid for asking a question to which everyone supposedly knew the answer. In other cases, I received a variety of pat answers, such as:

- To educate children
- To prepare young people for life in the twenty-first century
- To prepare young people for the world of work

In one instance, a teacher told me the mission of school was "to deliver the state-mandated curriculum to students."

In time it became obvious I was asking a question rarely asked by anyone. However, when pressed, even long-time educators had difficulty answering the question with any specificity and none of them came up with a response that was, in my mind, accurate or adequate.

The old adage, "If you don't know where you are going, any road will get you there," could apply to our schools. Without agreeing on the mission of school, it is impossible to generate a plan to make schools effective and to have them achieve their intended purpose.

Most people believe the mission of school is to educate children. However, that is so obvious it does not really tell us anything. It's like saying the mission of business is to make a profit. Both sound correct, but neither is a true mission. Rather, educating children and making a profit are goals. Neither goal defines the real purpose of the organization, nor does either provide the people working in it with a clear understanding of why the organization exists. All businesses want to make a profit, but they exist for totally different reasons. For example, if the mission of business was to make a profit, then the missions of Apple, General Motors, Holiday Inn, and the corner dry cleaner would all be the same. Of course, each of these businesses has a different mission even though they all share the same goal of wanting to be profitable.

In the same way, if the mission of school is to "educate children," then that applies equally to K–12 schools, Sunday schools, community colleges, universities, and the local karate studio. The term "educate children" does apply to all schools, but it is not a mission statement—it is a goal. It is also a goal of parents, or it should be. Moreover, what does it mean to "educate children?" *What is an educated child?*

Thus, the question stands: "What is the mission of school?" To answer that, one must first decide what the objective is and then decide what is required to meet that objective. A mission statement defines the purpose for an organization's existence. To be useful to the organization, the mission statement must be clear, concise, understood, and committed to by the members of the organization.

Since no one gave me an answer that I found useful, I developed my own. I thought about the role of public schools in our society, and how schools relate to what I believe we need to achieve through the education of our young people. I looked at the history of our schools and tried to assess what might have worked in the past, what is working now, and what is not working now. How did we turn out a Jefferson or a Lincoln without compulsory public schools? What is it that a person needs to learn to be considered educated? What role does school have in turning out educated adults? These and other similar questions influenced my thinking in developing a mission statement for school.

If the goal of school is to turn out an educated child, then we must define such a child. In other words, we must define what an educated child should know and be able to do, and we should know when we have achieved the goal.

## An Educated Child

IN 1992, the Secretary's Commission on Achieving Necessary Skills (SCANS) of the federal Department of Labor prepared a report on what young people would need to know and be able to do in order to be employable in the twenty-first century. That report suggested five mandatory skills.[1] Those skills were the ability to:

- Manage resources
- Work with others
- Acquire and use information
- Understand systems
- Use technology

Note: Some 27 years later, not a single state requires the mastery of even one of these skills in order to graduate from high school.

This list was perhaps influenced by an insightful article in *Fortune Magazine* (January 22, 1992), in which the authors suggested that an educated child would need to acquire the following skills and habits:[2]

- An ability to communicate effectively, orally and in writing
- A thorough grounding in literature and the social sciences, especially history and geography
- An understanding of the principles of higher mathematics, including the ability to apply those principles to daily life
- Knowledge of the physical sciences, including how these disciplines relate to the environment
- Mastery of at least one foreign language and culture
- Enough familiarity with computers and other technology to retrieve and use information easily
- An appreciation for the fine arts
- A genuine understanding of how the U.S. government and economy function
- Concern for physical health
- Above all else, the ability to identify problems and work creatively toward solutions

A few years later, Howard Gardner, in his book *Globalization: Culture and Education in the New Millennium*, suggested seven skills needed for life in the twenty-first century.[3] Those skills include an ability to:

- Understand global systems
- Think analytically and creatively within disciplines
- Tackle problems and issues that do not respect disciplinary boundaries
- Interact civilly and productively with individuals from different backgrounds—both within one's society and across the world
- Understand and respect their own cultural traditions
- Foster hybrid or blended identities—the ability to work, think and play across cultural boundaries
- Foster tolerance within and across nations

The above lists of skills represent some good thinking. The *Fortune Magazine* list strikes me as being the best and most complete. It delineates what a child would need to learn to be considered a well-educated person. Education scholars have updated and expanded this list to emphasize skills they deem important in this age of global commerce, but they tend to agree on key details. Based upon their scholarship and my own observations, I have developed the following list. Here is what I think a high school graduate needs to know and to be able to do in order to be considered "educated." The graduate must have:

- Communication skills:
  - Able to read, write, and speak the English language
  - Able to use technology to acquire and use information

- Citizenship skills:
  - Has an understanding of this country's history and the Constitution, has an appreciation of the right to vote, and intends to exercise that right
  - Has a basic understanding of economics and of how our economy works

- Global skills:
  - Has studied another language and culture
  - Has a reasonable understanding of world geography

- Math and science skills:
  - Can use and apply mathematical skills in daily life
  - Has an understanding of the physical sciences

- Personal qualities:
  - Does not lie, cheat, or steal
  - Appreciates the needs of others
  - Is understanding of differing viewpoints

• Has a good work ethic

• Takes responsibility for his or her own actions

• Has a basic understanding of the human body, knows what
good nutrition is and how to live a healthy life

David Brooks, in his book *The Social Animal*, asserts that *character* is a quality critical to the successful living of life. He describes people with character as being:

> energetic, honest and dependable. They were persistent after setback and acknowledged their mistakes. They possessed enough integrity to live up to their commitments. They tried to recognize their weaknesses, atone for their sins, and control their worst impulses.[4]

I like Brooks's definition of character and feel it is a good description of the personal qualities needed to live a successful life in a civilized society. Willard Daggett further reinforces this point in his paper on "Addressing the Issue of Character." There he notes:

> Whether we look at the basic characteristics of good citizenship from a democratic, religious, cultural or social/economic perspective, the same set of guiding principles keeps manifesting itself. Respect, responsibility, trustworthiness, loyalty, honesty, compassion, perseverance, courage, deliberateness, initiative, optimism and adaptability are all important qualities regardless of a person's gender or political, racial and religious convictions.[5]

Character education takes on even more importance when you look at the history of societies. As Lawrence W. Reed, President of the Foundation for Economic Education, states in his excellent article on the history of the Roman Empire:

> The paramount lesson of the Roman experience is actually not peculiar to Rome. It may be, in fact, the most universal lesson of all history: No people who have lost their character have kept their liberties.[6]

Brooks summarizes the discussion of character education by saying,

We are good at teaching technical skills, but when it comes to the most important things, like character, we have almost nothing to say.[7]

You will note there is nothing in my list of education skills and principles that relates to grade point averages or the number of degrees or letters that appear after a person's name. Society does not measure people that way, nor should it. Rather, society measures people based on character, on personality, on morals, on work ethic, on devotion to family, on patriotism, on civic-mindedness, and on overall preparedness for living in a civilized society.

Education provides preparation for life. It is about equipping a young person to live in our society and become a productive citizen. It is not about whether the child is good or bad at math or science, although those are important. It is about knowing how to live and to contribute, in the child's own way, to the betterment of our world.

A young person possessing the skills and attributes listed above is able to take care of himself or herself, is able to earn a living, will not be a burden on society, and accepts accountability and responsibility for his or her behavior. Such a person can best be described as a "responsible citizen." This being the case, then one of the missions of school is to turn out responsible citizens.

## Who Has the Responsibility?

WHO IS primarily responsible for the education of a child? Common wisdom suggests the school. Whenever student performance fails to meet expectations, parents, other citizens, policy makers, and the media first blame the schools, or teachers, or both. Schools definitely make an impact on student performance, but they are not where the primary blame belongs.

In 1992, President George H. W. Bush held an Education Summit in Charlottesville, Virginia, which Bill Clinton chaired. The summit resulted in a report, "Goals 2000."[8] The report included an amazing statistic. It stated that, "between birth and age 18, a young person will spend 90 percent of their life somewhere other than in school."[9]

Initially I didn't believe this figure, so I calculated it myself and came up with 89.7 percent. This profound statistic suggests that schools are only one component of a child's education, and not the most important component. The statistic shows that *the primary responsibility for the education of a child rests with the child's parents or guardians, not with the school.* It also shows that because parents and guardians have the primary responsibility for the education of their child, schools actually serve parents in the work of educating their child. *Expressed another way, parents are the customers of schools.*

This reasoning is not common in public education, but it has long been recognized by private schools. Private school parents are regarded not only as the primary source of funding, but also as the primary teachers of children. Private school teachers and administrators know that without extensive parental involvement in a child's education, that child will struggle. Successful public schools have also figured this out.

Children who have no parents or have parents unable or unwilling to participate in their child's education must receive such nurturing from another caring adult. Sometimes that is a grandparent, a neighbor, a teacher, or another adult who provides a positive daily influence on a child. Teachers in private boarding schools can fill this role, or they should. The involvement of a caring adult in a child's education is vital, and since schools only occupy 10 percent of a child's life, the caring adult's intervention can best be done at home. It is becoming increasingly obvious that no child can be adequately prepared for adulthood without the care, nurture, and love of an involved adult.

If parents are the primary educators of children, then schools, to be successful, must engage parents. They must treat parents as customers or partners and encourage parental involvement both at school and in the home. This reality is borne out of any analysis of high-performing schools, whether private or public. You will almost never find a high-performing school that does not have an inordinate amount of parental involvement. Such schools encourage, even demand, such involvement because they recognize the vital importance of parental participation in student learning.

This reality dictates how schools and districts must operate. They must cater to parents, meet parental requirements, and become parent-friendly. Smart schools and districts are creating *parent rooms* in schools. These rooms are designated for—and only for—parents to use during their school visits. Successful schools set goals for parental involvement and keep track of such involvement. Even in poverty-stricken neighborhoods, successful schools are able to engage parents in ways that are truly amazing. I have visited schools where welfare mothers, living in tenement housing, spend long hours in their children's school and come to believe that their children can be successful and that they, as parents, play an important role in making that happen.

Parents have many other partners who share in their responsibility—family members, friends, neighbors, peers, churches, synagogues, mosques, and, of course, schools. Of those, however, the primary partner is the school.

## The Mission

THUS, MY definition of the mission of a school recognizes the role of parents and the need to educate the child beyond the area of academics. My definition of the mission of a school is, then:

> *To serve as the primary partner, with parents, in the total development of their child into a responsible citizen.*

## Implications

FROM THIS mission statement, the following conclusions become obvious:

- The customer of a school is the parent, not the child, a labor union, or the government.

- Parental involvement is essential for the successful operation of a school and for the successful education of a child.
- Communication between parent and teacher is essential.
- Schools need to teach more than academics.
- Parents are the most important teachers of their child.

The above conclusions also show why neighborhood schools are so important. They are particularly important in urban neighborhoods where parents may not own a car and, therefore, may have difficulty becoming involved in their child's school if it is located a significant distance from the child's home.

Separation of parent and school by distance explains why mandatory busing, a social experiment, was unsuccessful. It failed, not because of racism (although race was certainly a factor), but because busing systematically removed parents from the education of their child and from involvement in their child's school.

I have come to the conclusion that the racial integration of our schools is really a question of parents' choosing where to live rather than being a social policy issue. There will always be concentrations of like people in specific neighborhoods. We saw that in various cities in the early years of our country's development. Italian people concentrated in one part of town, Irish people in another, and Polish people in still another. Most major cities have a Chinatown. This is normal and predictable.

Today, we see Korean neighborhoods, Vietnamese neighborhoods, Hispanic neighborhoods, etc. We have always had African-American neighborhoods, part of which was due to past racism, but part due to a desire to live near people of like backgrounds and culture. This concentration of similar people causes neighborhood schools to have concentrations of like types of students. This is to be expected and should not be discouraged or denied. Rather, parents must maintain control of where their child goes to school, and having that child as close to home as possible is beneficial to that child's education, particularly in the early grades. This belief will often yield highly concentrated populations of racially and/or ethnically similar children. Some call this the re-segregation of our schools. However, if a parent chooses the school closest to home and lives in a racially concentrated community, then that is not segregation; it is parental choice.

The important question is not, "Who is sitting next to my child in class?" but rather, "Is my child attending a quality school?" School districts, cities, and the courts should spend more time improving the quality of all schools rather than managing the racial, ethnic, or cultural makeup of particular student bodies. Also, total choice with a preference to the neighborhood school is, in my mind, the best type of "student assignment" policy to be employed by a school district.

## Role of the Parent

SCHOOLS MUST have parental involvement if they are to be successful in achieving their mission. In one elementary school I visited, there was a contract between the school and the parents. The school agreed to ensure that their child would perform at grade level or above in every subject, if the parents agreed that the child would come to school well-fed, clean, rested, and adequately clothed, that the parents would attend meetings at the school as requested, and that they would perform at home those tasks requested of them by the teachers. Parents were also asked to commit to reading to their child every day for at least 20 minutes.

This elementary school was located in a low-income neighborhood. The population of the school was 80 percent minority students, and over 70 percent of the student body qualified for free or reduced lunches (the definition used in education to define poverty). Yet the students did very well. There was high parental involvement and there were virtually no disciplinary problems.

## Total Development

I SELECTED the term *total development* very carefully. Total development means the child is taught values, learns right from wrong, acquires self-confidence, and can get along with others. The child also has a good work ethic, in addition to knowing math, science, English, reading, writing, and other subjects.

Total development cannot occur only in school, but it must be a part of school. Total development demands that the adults in school serve as excellent role models for the children. Teachers must help instill the traits needed for successful living. As we know, core habits of motivation, empathy, self-control, and persistence are necessary for living in our society and are also key components in a child's ability to learn. Self-discipline is more important than IQ when it comes to academic performance.[10] As Amanda Ripley puts it: "[C]onscientiousness—a tendency to be responsible, hard-working, and organized—matters at every point in the human life cycle. It even predicts how long people will live—with more accuracy than intelligence or background."[11]

## Responsible Citizen

THE TERM *responsible citizen* means that the child, upon graduation, is able to take care of himself or herself and will not become a burden to society. It means the child will enter adulthood capable of making a living or capable of continuing his or her formal education. It means that he or she recognizes personal ownership of behavior, self-management, and creating success. A responsible citizen is an adult knowledgeable enough about our country's history, government, Constitution, and economic system to be an informed voter. Finally, a responsible citizen is an adult capable of being a responsible parent.

## Conclusion

IF WE, as a society, could instill in our young people the skills and character traits listed above, we would have an educated, responsible electorate. We would reduce poverty and crime, and our country would become extraordinarily competitive in world markets. Our government would operate more effectively and efficiently, because there would be far fewer people dependent upon the social safety-net services provided by government.

This mission statement suggests that our schools should operate differently than they do today. Not only must schools recognize their role in the total development of a child; they must recognize the role of parents and of the community. They must be attuned to meeting the requirements of both the parents and the child. They must give parents greater opportunity and responsibility to be involved in their children's education.

Schools should become community learning centers where not only the child, but also the parents and members of the community, can gather to learn and to participate in the total development of the child. School employees must model behavior and structure that will enhance the total development of the child. Teachers and administrators need to understand that their role extends far beyond teaching a subject; they need to be teachers about life. They need to be role models in everything they do.

In summary, the mission of school can provide the very foundation upon which our society can be improved and rebuilt. It is obvious that our society has many problems today at all levels. It is equally obvious that the trouble starts early in life and continues from one generation to the next. If we can get back to basics by promoting personal accountability and by teaching strong character traits to our young people, in addition to academics, a multitude of other social ills will start to heal. Understanding the mission of school is the key starting point.

# 4. UNIONS AND CHANGE

UNIONS ARE OFTEN CRITICIZED AS THE BIGGEST OBSTACLE TO bringing real change in America's public schools. That criticism is largely justified. There are many cities in this country where the union leadership is much more interested in holding power than in educating children. However, asking unions to support or promote change is like asking water to flow uphill. Unions abhor change and will fight it with all the power they have, and they have a lot of power.

However, they did not start out as powerful entities. Unions derive their power from weak management. In fact, unions' strong position is the result of management failure. One need only look at the history of the labor movement, at any industry where unions are strong, to find workers who felt a need to organize in order to obtain reasonable wages, fair treatment, and better working conditions. As workers, teachers are no different.

The bigger question is: How do we create an environment where unions and management can work together? Even better, how do we create an environment where the workers do not feel the need for a union? If we already have a union, how do we act as one unit and/or how do we develop a school system where teachers are not forced, or don't feel a need, to belong to a union?

For the first half of the twentieth century, the power over schools rested with the administrators and school boards. Teachers had little say and were not organized in any way. In those days, teaching was the primary employment opportunity for women. Some teachers were treated well, and some were not. Compensation was quite variable, as were working conditions. After World War II, as unions gained strength in other industries, teachers began to organize. In the 1960s, this was made easier as both states and the federal government enacted laws that allowed, and in some cases encouraged, public employees to engage in collective bargaining. Terry Moe writes:

> By the time the dust settled in the early 1980s, virtually all districts of any size (outside the South) were successfully organized, collective bargaining was the norm, and the teachers unions reigned supreme as the most powerful force in American education.[1]

Over the years, unions have been successful in raising teacher compensation, improving teacher working conditions, and protecting teacher employment. That is their job and they do it well. However, in protecting the economic interests of teachers, they have handcuffed effective managers, blocked positive change, and resolutely preserved the status quo. They have done this so well, in fact, that public education has seen little meaningful reform in the last 50 years.

Since 1980, union membership has grown fastest in the public sector. A large portion of city, county, state, and federal workers across the country are now members of collective bargaining units. Public education, as an arm of government, fits into this category. Today, even in "Right to Work" states, education unions are powerful elements of the education workforce. Unions, as one would expect, are strongest where management has been weakest and most compliant.

Conversely, unions have declined dramatically in the private sector. In private companies, managers have become more sophisticated and more conscious that taking care of employees is as important as taking care of their customers. In fact, one concern begets the other. Wherever you see excellent managers, you will generally see weak unions or no unions at all. Workers, in a well-managed organization, do not need a union in order to have good working conditions, competitive compensation, and job security. However, a well-managed organization provides those conditions only when performance by the worker is satisfactory. In these types of organizations, there is no protection for incompetence, nor is there a seniority-based guarantee of employment. Employees in these organizations must continue to contribute in order to maintain their positions.

Public education has not worked that way, but it should. Today, teachers and principals often receive tenure after only three years on the job. Once tenure is achieved, it becomes very difficult to dismiss a teacher or principal, regardless of their inability to perform their job. This situation perpetuates mediocrity, which hurts the education of children.

Joel Klein, former chancellor of the New York City Schools, described union effectiveness this way:

> [U]nion members... want lifetime job security (tenure), better pay regardless of performance (seniority pay), less work (short days, long holidays, lots of sick days), and the opportunity to retire early (at, say, 55) with a good lifetime pension and full health benefits; for their part, the retirees want to make sure their benefits keep coming and grow through cost-of-living increases. The result: whether you work hard or don't, get good results with kids or don't, teach in a shortage area like math or special education or don't, or in a hard-to-staff school in a poor community or not, you get paid the same, unless you've been around for another year, in which case you get more. Not bad for adults... disastrous for kids in our schools.[2]

Some years ago, I had lunch with the president of the state teachers union in Washington State, the Washington Education Association (WEA). During our lunch, I asked her, "What is the mission of the union?" She was somewhat taken aback by the question, but said, "The mission of the union is the education of children, of course." I told her I disagreed. We discussed the issue for over an hour, and when we finished, she agreed that the mission of the union was:

- To maximize member compensation
- To improve member working conditions
- To secure and protect member employment

I agreed with that definition of her union's mission. I also agreed that they had done a magnificent job of achieving their mission, but noted that it was done at the expense of our children. Even though the union had been successful in achieving their mission, I pointed out that it was the wrong mission. I said that because there is increasing concern about the performance of our schools and their ability to educate our children. Test scores have not changed, drop-out rates have not changed, and the achievement gap (the difference in test scores between whites and minorities) has not changed. Pressure to reform the system is escalating and will not subside until progress is made. So I suggested to her that until and unless the union focuses on furthering the interests of children, not adults, it would be unsuccessful in effectively educating every child, which is what their mission should be. What it should do, as an organization, is focus on the teaching effectiveness of every union member to ensure the effective education of every child. If they did that, the union could achieve its mission on behalf of its members. High-performing schools attract students, and that increases the number of teachers, which in turn, increases union membership and dues.

The three elements of the union mission described above all focus on the needs and desires of adults, while public schools need to focus on the needs and learning requirements of children. Thus, there is an inherent conflict that arises every time union representatives and school managers gather to negotiate. The union negotiators focus on the needs or perceived needs of its members, and school managers must focus on the needs of parents and students, who are their customers.

School managers also need to be concerned about the needs of employees in order to be successful at meeting customer requirements. When that occurs, the organization flourishes. When it doesn't occur, you see strong unions and, more often than not, poor-quality education for children.

This tension plays out in public schools and in government agencies. You also saw it in the automobile industry. Auto manufacturing, one of the most heavily unionized industries in our country, had some of the most worker-focused contracts ever negotiated. However, those labor contracts could not protect the workers from marketplace competition as car buyers found they could buy a better car and/or a less-expensive car from foreign manufacturers. The result was a rapid decline in the size and market share of domestic manufacturers which reduced employment in the auto industry. Today, the United Auto Workers (UAW) has more than one million fewer members than it had in the 1979.[3] Schools are witnessing the same trend, as private and charter schools grow and take market share from public schools. This trend will continue unless public school managers and local unions focus on their collective customers—parents and students.

Over the decades, public school teachers unions have been able to secure extensive management concessions, strict grievance procedures, generous sick leave and union leave provisions, rich benefit packages, stringent work rules, and tenure. In most cases, these broad economic entitlements for adults have dramatically increased the cost of operating public schools—thereby alienating taxpayers—and have not enhanced student academic achievement. These economic gains were conceded by weak management (superintendents and school boards) and by the increasing power of the unions. Contract terms, over the years, have been built upon until they have become a major constraint to the effective operation of schools.

A report by the *Education Partnership* (March 2005) points out that union contracts have now arrived at a point where they consistently:[4]

- Restrict flexibility and school autonomy
- Drive up the cost of education without improving quality
- Entrench the role of the union position in labor contracts, weakening management rights

The report further states that union contracts are filled with "the micromanagement of teachers, limitations to instructional time, generous paid time-off, incredible health and retirement packages, teacher transfer and assignment rights, limits to evaluation of teachers and numerous other stipulations." It then adds: "Many of these contract mandates limit the ability of teachers to perform as professionals and serve their students, and the authority of administrators to get the most out of the public's education dollars."[5]

Weak management deserves a strong union, but as management improves, contract terms become a constraint in improving the operation of any organization, including public schools. The base union contract for Seattle Public Schools is 202 pages long and its terms reflect decades of mistrust. It is the most limiting and onerous employment agreement I have ever read. The table of contents of the current contract is attached as Appendix A and will provide you with an overview of the complexity of this employment agreement. This contract is not dissimilar to contracts in other urban school systems. In fact, the larger the district, the more extensive are the contract terms.

As we endeavor to improve our schools, the dominant position of unions within public education must change. However, you cannot expect unions to lead this change, as their job is to protect the interests, compensation, and employment of their members. Union leaders will not willingly give up hard-won provisions of a labor contract.

Nor can superintendents or school boards expect a local union to support change just because they believe it to be in the best interest of children. Rather, school boards and superintendents must first regain trust from the district employees and the community at large. This requires excellent people in both positions. Without effective leadership and stable governance, unions will not only continue to resist change but also ensure that reform decisions made by management are not implemented.

Implementing change will require leadership that gains the trust not only of public education employees and the community but also of union leadership. That can be difficult because management and unions are seldom in agreement on any substantive issue. Management generally wants more production for less money, and unions want more money for less work. It is a built-in conflict. The problem is obvious and, therefore, can be dealt with.

The best example I can give of how change can be made, even with a strong union, is the experience of Seattle in 1996–97. In September of 1995, while serving on the school board, my colleagues and I had appointed John Stanford, a former Army Major General, as superintendent. One of his first initiatives was to connect personally with the teachers employed by the District. He would visit area schools every morning, four days a week. He was the first modern-day superintendent to visit all 96 of Seattle's public schools in one year. His visits included not only meeting with the principals, but also visiting classrooms, where he would talk with and listen to teachers. He would empathize with them over the daily challenges they faced and promised to work to correct problems. He also connected with the children. He urged them to work hard, to listen to their teachers, to come to school every day and to strive to do their best. This personal concern for students endeared him to parents as well.

As Superintendent Stanford toured area schools, he discussed with union representatives ways to improve teacher performance. He wanted union leaders to know he was concerned about ensuring every child was taught by a competent teacher. For their part, union leaders felt the problem faced by teachers was more about the competence of principals than about teacher performance. The union's concern was to protect its members from the unfair decisions of incompetent principals. For this reason a serious impasse developed.

Superintendent Stanford, who expected the same high performance from principals as he did from teachers, decided to invite the union to become a partner with school district management in improving the quality of all employees—teachers, principals, support staff, and others.

Washington State is one of the most heavily unionized states in the country. Unions hold political power at all levels of government, and they fight any and all efforts to reduce their dominant status. Given this situation, it was obvious that the only way to bring positive change to schools, at the district level, was to do so in concert with the union and not attempt to force change against organized labor's wishes. It was equally obvious the changes we wished to implement could not succeed without the union's concurrence.

At the time of Superintendent Stanford's appointment, principals in Seattle Public Schools exercised no authority over staff, money, or curriculum. They were, however, expected to be accountable to the public and to the school board for the educational performance of their schools. It was an impossible situation, and both Superintendent Stanford and we, on the school board, knew it. We felt each local principal, in order to be professionally accountable to us, needed to have staffing authority, budgetary authority, and operational authority over his or her own school. With such authority granted locally, the superintendent would be in a position to measure the effectiveness of each principal and could then weed out incompetent managers.

We thus concurred with our union that we first had to improve the professional competence of principals before we could set accountability expectations for teachers. To make that happen, we had to change the job description of the principal by building in local accountability for staff selection and performance, budget preparation, spending and student learning. This required a change in the union contract with regard to staffing rules and a change in how we allocated money to schools. Superintendent Stanford, with the blessing of the school board, approached the union with a plan.

Our proposal was that the school district would agree to get rid of incompetent principals, in return for union support in bringing about needed change. The job description of a principal had to be modified to give principals specific accountability, which meant that principals had to be given authority over the hiring of staff, the expenditure of money, and the rules for operating their building.

The union was very supportive of management's intention to dismiss incompetent principals and supported that effort. Union leaders reluctantly came to understand that, in order for principals to be accountable, principals needed to be given the level of the authority we proposed. Thus, the issue of employee seniority came immediately to the forefront of our discussions. If we were to give our principals authority to hire the teachers they wanted, they could not continue to be obligated to hire blindly on the basis of teacher seniority. Obviously, the union was against this proposal. Teacher seniority is a sacred job security policy of unions, and for them to give it up would be to act against everything they stood for.

The district was adamant that seniority rules had to be relaxed in order to create accountability for principals, which itself was a prerequisite to management's being able to terminate incompetent principals. The union was equally adamant that seniority was a job-protection rule they could not give up. The two parties were at an impasse.

After much frank negotiating and the establishment of trust between management and the union, an agreement was reached that worked for both parties. The union agreed to eliminate seniority as the basis for hiring teachers, in exchange for the creation of a *leadership team* in each building. In practice, each school would create a leadership team made up of six employees, working in the building, elected by their peers. This team of six people would work with the principal in the selection and hiring of new teaching staff, in setting rules for the daily operation of the building and in the preparation of the school budget. The board and superintendent agreed to this provision, provided the final decision on all these matters would rest with the principal. The union reluctantly agreed!

A new contract was prepared and signed by union representatives and district management. This was a landmark achievement, and three years later, when the labor contract was up for renewal, the issue of seniority in hiring was not even a subject of discussion. In the intervening three years, the leadership team concept had worked so well that teachers in each school wanted to retain their new authority. They obviously liked being able to help select the people with whom they would work.

From the principal's point of view, the arrangement made managing daily operations easier and more effective. More of the teaching staff was involved in making key decisions, and staff competence improved along with staff morale. It was a true win-win situation. This agreement took place in 1997.

The above experience is a classic example of how effective school district management can work with unions to initiate change. A successful process starts with trust, and then requires agreement on a common outcome. In this case, the union wanted the district to rid itself of incompetent principals (no principal had been fired in the previous 25 years) and the district wanted to change the job of the principal so that it would encompass the accountability needed to evaluate performance and, if necessary, terminate incompetent principals. The net effect of the new union agreement was the dismissal of four principals, followed by that of three other principals the following year. Other principals chose to leave the district, or retire, as they were not comfortable with their new authority and accountability. Many did not want to be held accountable for their school's performance. Conversely, principals from all over the country started applying to work in Seattle Public Schools.

Over a period of five years following the ratification of this new contract, the school district replaced 70 of the 96 principals. After these changes had occurred, the union had very few complaints about the competency of the leadership working in school buildings.

Not only was the school district able to upgrade the quality of principals, but principals in turn dramatically improved the quality of teachers working in the schools. Really good principals will not tolerate incompetent teachers. Nor will they tolerate teachers who chose not to adapt to the culture and/or the goals of the building. For this reason, many teachers left the district, or transferred to schools within the district where their particular approach to teaching was more compatible with the manner in which that school was being operated. Again, the voluntary movement of teaching personnel created a win-win situation for the school employees, for the students, and for public education.

This change in the contract allowed the union to achieve some of its goals as well. Working conditions improved for the teachers. Local schools received new and better leaders, teachers had more input to how the school operated, and staff morale improved.

Children also benefited as the schools began to operate more effectively. This resulted in increased test scores, reduced dropout rates, and a dramatic decrease in violence and disruptions. Also, the voters started passing levies that had formerly been defeated. The ultimate impact was an increase in the student population of the district, as parents began to believe in Seattle Public Schools again. The net effect was the hiring of more teachers to handle increased enrollment (thus increasing union membership and dues), another win for the union.

I should point out that one of the reasons why all this occurred was the charismatic leadership of Superintendent John Stanford. He had practically become a folk hero in Seattle, and the public was behind virtually anything he wanted to do. The union knew this and knew that if John Stanford felt he needed to eliminate seniority in the hiring of teachers, and if he went to the public with that issue, the public would very likely support him and not the union. Even though the solution was a win-win for the union and the district, I believe it would not have happened without truly competent leadership at the superintendent level and at the board level.

Between 1968 and the early 1990s, Seattle Public Schools dropped in enrollment from 100,000 children to 39,000. Today, there are 53,000 students attending public schools in Seattle. That earlier drop in student enrollment reduced teacher employment by over 4,000. It also reduced union membership by the same amount. When a union loses members, it loses dues revenue. In other words, contracted job security cannot be accomplished in education any more than it could in the automobile industry.

Job security is accomplished only by meeting customer (parent and student) requirements. As schools improve, parents will bring their children back to the district. Not only are teachers retained but new ones are hired, and everyone in the system achieves their goals—including the economic goals of the union. In Seattle, our union leaders understood this reality, and, once they did, a partnership was established that helped the district, the union and the students of Seattle succeed.

A postscript to this story is the sad and early death of John Stanford, in 1998, due to cancer. He was a dynamic leader, and, without a similar leader, the public support for the schools started to wane. By 2003, less than 5 years after his passing, the district became embroiled in a crippling financial scandal, the voters elected a new, activist board, the succeeding superintendent was removed, and trust between the school system and the union began to decline. Over the following ten years, the district experienced five superintendents, high turnover in school board membership, and variable and unstable support from parents. By 2005, student enrollment had again declined and is only now starting to recover. In 2011, seven public schools were closed amid much community acrimony. In 2015, the union held a one-week strike over wages and working conditions. In 2019, district relations with the teachers union can be described as only fair, and the school board has now hired the sixth superintendent in ten years.

The difficulty of maintaining reform is not unique to Seattle. It happens time and again in communities throughout the country. In fact, few urban districts have been able to sustain a long-term effort for school improvement. Education leaders in New York, Boston, and Chicago are trying, but with only limited success so far. Even when effective leadership is present, change is not sustainable, because dynamic leaders move on, but the local union remains. Washington, DC, under the leadership of Michelle Rhee, was the most aggressive at changing the system, but her constructive reforms were soon stopped, and in some cases reversed, by the union's ability to unseat her political protector, Mayor Fantey.

Over the years, union power has substantially increased to the point where it now influences elections at the national, state, and local levels. Today, labor unions have more influence on the public schools than any other group in American society, including voters.[6] As education policy analyst Terry Moe puts it:

> Their influence takes two forms. They shape schools from the bottom up, through collective bargaining activities so broad in scope that virtually every aspect of school organization bears the distinctive imprint of union design. They also shape the schools from the top down, through political activities that give them unrivaled influence over the laws and regulations imposed on public education by Government, that allow them to block or weaken governmental reforms they find threatening. In combining bottom-up and top-down influence, and in combining them as potently as they do, the teachers unions are unique among all actors in the educational area.[7]

Unions have an additional advantage unique to education. Because all districts are mandated to provide 180 days of schooling per year, the threat of a strike does not incur any economic disadvantage to teachers. If they go on strike, the school year is simply extended. Thus, there is no penalty to the worker as there is in other industries. Teachers can be out for weeks without losing any income because the school year is simply extended by the length of the strike. Also, a strike quickly alienates the parent community. Parents have to scramble to find daycare services or baby-sitters for their children while the parent is at work. This causes the parent community to immediately put pressure on school boards to settle any dispute. Parents don't care how much the union is requesting, they just want their children back in school. These two factors give unions enormous power, and this can dramatically reduce the impact of effective leadership. Often, just the threat of a strike is enough for the unions to achieve their goals.

Today, the National Education Association (NEA) is the largest union in the country and has the most influence on political races throughout the nation. Combined with the American Federation of Teachers (AFT), the two labor organizations have a combined membership of "well over 4 million."[8]

In the roughly twenty-year period from 1989 to 2010, these two unions were the largest political contributors to candidates in federal elections.[9] They are also powerful contributors in local and state elections and, as can be seen in almost any city, can strongly influence, and almost determine, the outcome of local school board elections. In fact, these two unions can influence and have influenced elections at every level of public office, and, as long as they retain their power, every indication is that they will continue to do so.

The bottom line is that the opposition of teachers unions is a major force to contend with in the ongoing effort to improve our public schools. They know their mission and they carry it out admirably. If we are serious about fixing our public schools, we will have to ultimately deal with the power of unions, but that can only occur after we have improved the competency of education management, not only at the school and district level, but at the state level as well.

There is no doubt that unions impose a major constraint on efforts to improve our schools, but that constraint can be accommodated if there is effective leadership at the principal, superintendent, and board levels of management. Permanently reducing the negative impact of unions on the effective education of our children can occur only through a radical increase in the competency of leadership in our schools, cities, and states. Working on improving leadership is a basic requirement of mitigating union opposition to constructive change.

In the past few years, we have seen the power of leadership exercised at the state level, particularly in Wisconsin and Indiana. Former Governors Scott Walker and Mitch Daniels exercised enormous leadership related to unions. Daniels managed to pass a Right-To-Work law in

Indiana, and Walker managed to remove mandated union membership for government employees and passed Right-To-Work legislation. These legislative changes have allowed schools in Wisconsin to become the equivalent of charter schools, as each school is now free to hire only the best teachers and reward excellence in teaching, if they so choose. The net effect is that education costs have declined, schools have improved, and both the parents and taxpayers have come out ahead. In addition, I am certain that the teachers are finding their new freedom invigorating. In fact, more than half the teachers in Wisconsin have given up their union membership.[10] Again, fixing leadership, at all levels, is the primary way to combat the power of unions.

Sometimes it can be necessary to use other means to combat the power of unions. The very recent (June 2014) court ruling in *Vergara v. California* is an example where the courts can be helpful in reducing the power of unions. This case pertained to the right of students to have access to quality teachers. Nine students, from poverty neighborhood schools, filed the case to overturn the seniority and tenure laws that offer job security to educators. Their contention was that these laws prevented them from having equal access to quality teachers. The court agreed with their argument and ruled both laws unconstitutional, a huge win for students, for parents, and for quality teachers.

This is a landmark decision that will have ramifications well beyond the State of California. More state legislatures will be looking at seniority and tenure as questionable contract terms and assessing their impact on student achievement.

However, even the elimination of seniority and tenure will not totally dissolve the power of unions. They are still going to wield tremendous power that will continue to handcuff our school systems. This court decision will cause them to work even harder to solidify their position. As a consequence, effective leadership becomes even more essential. Improving the quality of management and leadership of our schools and of our state governments is still an essential step in improving our schools.

Though unions are, in my mind, the major constraint upon improving our schools, they are not the source of the problem—management is! And here, management refers not only to school and district management but to state and federal management as well. Leadership needs to improve at all levels and laws need to be changed before we can hope to diminish the power of unions. As I said earlier, unions are the result of management failure. If you want to reduce the power of unions, fix management!

Fixing management is going to take time and, in the meantime, work on improving our schools needs to focus on those states where union power has been mitigated by state law. There are now 28 states that have passed "Right-To-Work" legislation. It is in those states that immediate change can begin.

To mitigate the power of unions, state legislatures should pass "Right-to-Work" legislation, provide parents with choice in the selection of the school their children attend, and change the way we select and train leaders for our schools. Of these three things, the last may be the most important.

On June 27, 2018, the United States Supreme Court ruled in the *Janus* case, to outlaw mandatory union membership for government employees. This change in Federal Law could, over time, dramatically reduce the power of unions. As we saw in Wisconsin, after the passage of similar legislation for that state, the teacher's union lost 60% of its membership and, therefore, sixty percent of its revenues. The same outcome is now possible in every state. If this were to occur, we would see major changes in school operations and in employment practices.

However, the unions have witnessed what occurred in Wisconsin and are aggressively working to retain membership in spite of the new law. Since unions have continued to exist and have power in "Right-to-Work" states, we should not expect them to go away simply because they have lost their monopoly position (mandatory union membership as a condition of employment). In fact, we can expect them to be even more aggressive in their efforts to retain membership and to enhance the value they provide their members.

Also, even with this change in the law, the power of unions can still be retained if the quality of leadership does not improve. High-quality teachers will not work for low-quality or mediocre principals and, if teachers find themselves in that situation, they will want a union, as well they should.

Thus, though unions have lost their monopoly position, they have not lost their reason for existing. As pointed out earlier, unions are the result of management failure. Even with the new law, that point is still valid. Thus, to mitigate both the need for and the power of unions, we need to dramatically improve leadership. We'll discuss that issue in Chapter 6.

# PART TWO:
# STEPS FOR CHANGE

# 5. Teaching

IN MANY OF MY SPEECHES ON EDUCATION, I WOULD START BY ASKING a question: "How many of you can recall one teacher who made a positive difference in your education and, perhaps, in the person you have become?" Almost every hand in the room would go up. I would then ask, "How many of you can remember two teachers who made a positive difference in your life?" About half the hands would go up. I would then ask, "How many of you can recall three such teachers?" About 10 percent of the hands would go up.

What is interesting about this is that, in our K–12 schooling years, each of us probably had 30 to 35 teachers. In other words, most of us cannot remember or were not materially influenced by over 90 percent of the teachers we had in school. This is a pretty sad statistic, but it is the way school was for most of us. This may say something about our poor memories, but it says far more about the quality of our teachers. When we were fortunate enough to be assigned to a gifted teacher, that person positively influenced us, often for life.

No matter how many research papers you read about teaching, the one universal truth is that quality teaching yields quality learning for students. Studies have shown that if you take high-performing students and put them in a classroom with a low-performing teacher, they will soon become low-performing students. Conversely, if you put low-performing students in a classroom with a high-performing teacher, they will become high-performing students. Parents matter most, but then teachers.[1]

Kati Haycock of the Education Trust says:

A decade ago… we believed that what students learned was largely a factor of their family income or parental education, not of what schools did. But recent research has turned these assumptions upside down.

What schools do matters—enormously. And what matters most is good teaching.[2]

In other words, how well a child learns in school is primarily determined by the quality of the teacher in the classroom.

Data tells us that a quality teacher can overcome the effects on students of a poor home environment. A good teacher can allow a child to succeed in class, in spite of the social and economic circumstances into which the child was born.

Great teachers can make miracles happen. They are, perhaps, the most important members of our society. When students receive excellent teaching, year after year, they flourish. If a student receives poor teaching for only a few years, that child's education will be permanently damaged. This point is corroborated by research done in Tennessee schools that showed a fourfold increase in learning achievement by students who had a series of excellent teachers compared to students of similar backgrounds who had a series of poor teachers.[3]

Poor-quality teaching or inadequate teaching has a huge economic impact as well. Universities and community colleges have to provide hours of remedial classes for a large percentage of their entering students. Businesses suffer by not having available the trained people needed to staff their operations. Our overall prosperity suffers, and the cost to the economy runs into billions of dollars.[4]

Eric Hanushek, of Stanford University's Hoover Institution, estimates that a significant improvement in education, over a 20-year period, could lead to as much as a four-percentage-point boost in the Gross Domestic Product. In today's terms, that would be over $800 billion in economic growth a year, an amount that rivals total current spending on K–12 public education.

The future of this country depends on our having a well-educated citizenry. To make that a reality, we must have excellent schools available to all children. As one respected national report put it:

Top-quality teaching fosters high student achievement—and high achievers can harness their talents and energies to become successful, contributing citizens.[5]

Given the validity of that statement, it would seem reasonable to expect a country to treat teaching as a high-status profession. Yet, here in America, we do anything but. We continue to "treat teaching—the profession that makes all other professions possible—as a second-rate occupation."[6]

The Education Trust puts it this way:

Nearly 200,000 graduates from schools of education and those who have completed alternative route teaching programs are placed in American classrooms each year. Too often, these educators, and the school districts that hire them, find out all too soon that they are ill-prepared for the demands of today's classrooms. As a consequence, the children in their classes do not have the opportunity to learn to high levels. This practice is unfair to teachers and devastating to students, especially to students of color, low-income students, English language learners, and students with disabilities, who year after year are taught by the least effective teachers.[7]

The lack of emphasis on teaching is one of the reasons our children are not performing at levels that are competitive with other countries. Though substantial increases in funding of education have occurred in the past several decades, student test scores are still about the levels they were in 1970. Moreover, we face a significant ethnicity gap. The Education Trust reports that 33 of every 100 white students who enter kindergarten will graduate from college, but only 18 of every 100 African-American kindergartners will earn a similar degree. Hispanic children have comparable statistics.[8] An increasing number of today's jobs require at least a two-year advanced degree in order for an applicant to qualify for a position. The above dismal performance, for white, black, and Hispanic students does not come close to meeting the demands of society. If the level of learning cannot be increased, this country will rapidly lose its position as a world economic leader and the standard of living for our citizens will decline. This prediction is already coming true for an increasing number of our citizens.

The quality of teaching matters! In fact, all other factors pale in comparison. So how are we doing in attracting and retaining excellent teachers?

Today, a third of teachers entering the profession will leave before they complete their fifth year in the classroom. In large urban systems, fully half of their teachers will leave within five years. In some of those districts, half leave within three years.[9] Moreover, the first teachers to leave the profession tend to be those who had the best SAT scores when entering college.[10] Though a high SAT score is not a guarantee of teaching success, it is a good indicator of a person's verbal and cognitive skills. Studies show that teachers with strong verbal and cognitive ability are most likely to improve student achievement.[11] In fact, a teacher's verbal and cognitive ability has a greater impact on student learning than any other measured characteristic.[12]

The departure of large numbers of teachers, particularly the brightest, has created a competency crisis in our schools. This crisis will only get worse over the next decade, because our country will need to add two million new teachers, almost half of whom will be needed in urban areas.

So we have a national situation in which the most important profession in our society is experiencing high turnover, and is losing its best people the fastest. Moreover, the vast majority of our best and brightest people don't even consider entering the profession of teaching.

Some would argue that the reason the best and brightest young people do not seek to become teachers is the amount of money we pay our teachers. I'm sure that is one consideration, but later I will discuss teacher compensation and why it is not the overriding reason our brightest people do not enter the profession. I would argue that we have so few gifted teachers partly because of the many new career opportunities now open to women, but primarily because of the restrictive laws and regulations governing teaching that make it an unattractive profession.

Getting the best teachers requires that we encourage the best students from our universities and the best people from our society to go into teaching. That does not occur in our present education system. Richard F. Elmore puts it this way:

> Today, we have a cartel that controls the supply of human capital that is allowed into our schools. This cartel consists of "state agencies, cash-for-credit university programs and hopelessly inadequate local hiring practices."[13]

To overcome these problems and improve the quality of our teaching corps, we must address three issues:

1.  Selection and Preparation
2.  Placement and Working Conditions
3.  Compensation

All three areas require major changes if we truly expect to make teaching a real profession and to have our brightest citizens enter and spend at least several years in the teaching field.

## 1. Selection and Preparation

PROFESSIONALS IN areas of law, medicine, engineering, etc., are carefully selected prior to being accepted into a college program. They then go through extensive educational training followed by on-the-job training. New lawyers come into law firms and work directly under a partner or other experienced lawyer. Doctors graduate from medical school and serve an extensive internship prior to practicing medicine on their own. Engineers join an engineering firm, continue their training and then take an exam to get licensed. Certified public accountants do much the same. Professors in universities conduct extensive study in their area of expertise before applying for faculty positions. Would-be professors must prove they possess a deep knowledge of a subject area and have an ability to teach it effectively to college students.

In each case, the individual is carefully selected (only the best and brightest are accepted) and must receive extensive training beyond the classroom to prove qualification before being allowed to practice.

However, entry into teaching is not done that way. All a teacher-to-be has to do is get accepted into an education school, which is the easiest college on a campus to get into. For most of these schools, the requirement for entry is a high school diploma and money for tuition. If a young person possesses those two attributes, he or she can be accepted into an education school. Once accepted, they spend four years taking courses in the curriculum required by the chosen school of education. This rather bizarre reality is the result of our state teacher-certification laws. The narrow cartel mentioned above is the direct result of these restrictive laws. Certification laws were supposedly designed to ensure that only "qualified" teachers entered our classrooms. Requiring that teachers be officially certified, it was argued, would ensure that only high-quality instruction was allowed in the classroom. In the early years, this was probably the case. However, today these well-intentioned laws are a large stumbling block to real improvement in our teaching force.

These laws required the creation of schools of education at universities and colleges throughout the country. Education schools were established for the purpose of developing the art and science of teaching. Professors for these schools were drawn from other disciplines of the university. Graduates of these schools would then be "certified" teachers thoroughly familiar with their subject area and competent to teach it.

Initially, schools of education were well-staffed and the professional training they provided was on a par with other academic disciplines within the university.

However, in addition to the formation of schools of education, state certification laws mandated that public school administrators could hire only officially certified teachers, that is, only those who had attended and completed the course of study at an approved school of education. I am sure that in the early years, this requirement was useful in improving the teaching profession. However, today that is no longer the case.

Laws that mandated the hiring of only certified teachers resulted in giving schools of education monopoly control over the supply of human capital entering our public schools. Like any monopoly, over time the business of certifying teachers became bureaucratized, bloated, inefficient, and ineffective. Today, there are over 1,400 schools that are licensed to grant teacher certifications and the spectrum of quality between the best and the worst is substantial.

In most schools of education, teachers-in-training take courses in pedagogy, lesson planning, mathematics, social studies, etc. Student teachers are routinely given instruction on the latest in teaching trends, but, in many cases, they are not required to demonstrate mastery of the subject they plan to teach. Elementary-level teachers receive instruction on how to teach reading, but they do not have to prove an ability to do so. Similarly, secondary-level teachers do not have to show an ability to teach the specific subject of their choice, such as math, English, or science. As a consequence, teachers at any level who plan to teach in a specific subject area do not have to demonstrate academic mastery of that subject.

In 2006, Dr. Arthur Levine, former president of Teachers College, Columbia University, published a scathing report on our nation's schools of education.[14] Dr. Levine describes schools of education as "programs that teach outdated curricula and [have] failed to keep pace with demographics, technology, global competition and pressures to raise student achievement."[15] He also states that "universities have exacerbated the situation by continuing to treat teacher-preparation programs as 'cash cows,' leading them to set low admission and graduation standards for their students."[16]

This latter point is particularly important, because most schools of education have, over time, become an important source of revenue to their host university. By setting low admission standards, they are catering to our least-qualified young people. In many universities, the program with the lowest average student SAT scores is the school of education. "One study found that college graduates, whose SAT or ACT scores were in the bottom quartile, were more than twice as likely as those in the top quartile to have majored in education."[17] Another study found that just 14 percent of college graduates with a major in education had SAT or ACT scores in the top quartile.[18]

Education schools are not the only problem. Many states have alternative certification programs that provide certification to students who have never attended an education school.

> The U.S. Department of Education found in 2013–14 that of the 37,270 individuals enrolled in teacher-training programs in Texas, more than 15,000 were in alternative programs unaffiliated with any university. Many new teachers point and click their way to certification over the internet without ever setting foot in a classroom, and circumvent university preparation completely.
>
> According to the federal Education Department's 2015 Title II report, Texas gave authority for teacher certification to 199 entities in 2013–14—including regional service centers, community colleges and for profit businesses—which offer about 6,000 different programs.
>
> Policies in states like Texas allow anyone and everyone to teach, even the woefully unqualified and the blatantly unprepared. Standards for teacher quality have gotten so low that they are no longer meaningful.[19]

Our society clearly needs the best and brightest people to go into teaching, and that is not occurring. To change this situation, we must remove, or radically modify, our state certification laws. I'm not suggesting that we eliminate schools of education, but we must induce them to prove their ability to train and graduate effective teachers. By eliminating their monopoly position, schools of education would have to do just that. The net effect would be the closure of some schools of education and the dramatic restructuring of others. Both outcomes would be of benefit to our children's education.

The idea of repealing state certification laws is not as radical as it may seem. Most faculty members at schools of education are themselves not certified. Nor are their peers in the other programs of a university. University professors are not required to be "certified" under state law. Nor are the faculty members of community colleges or private K–12 schools. The only education organization in our entire society that is restricted by law to hiring only teachers approved by an official school of education is our public schools. Another bizarre fact is that fewer than half of our schools of education, only 550 out of 1,400, are accredited (assuming for the moment that school accreditation has any more validity than teacher certification). This double weakness (uncertified professors in unaccredited schools) means that many, perhaps most, teachers are certified by an educational process presented by uncertified staff in unaccredited institutions.[20]

Current certification laws focus on ensuring that new teachers spend a fixed number of hours studying at a school of education. The laws do not focus on professional competency, nor do they specify that new teachers must show mastery of subject matter. Certification laws are very much like many graduation requirements; the focus is on student "seat time" rather than learning.

Today, in education schools, we try to teach students how to teach content, instead of training content-competent people how to teach. We have it backwards.

This has created the following situation in our country. Having highly qualified teachers for every class is especially problematic when the current science and mathematics teachers in the profession do not have science or mathematics backgrounds. Approximately 25 percent of high school mathematics teachers and 20 percent of high school science teachers don't have even a minor degree in their teaching field.[21]

Because of the shortage of science and mathematics teachers, licensed teachers in other subject areas are often asked to teach science or mathematics. For 56 percent of high school students taking physical science classes and 27 percent of high school students taking mathematics classes, their teachers are teaching out-of-field. These percentages are higher in high-poverty schools."[22]

Students cannot learn from teachers who don't know their subject. This is especially true in math and science. "About two-thirds of the students studying chemistry and physics in U.S. high schools are taught by teachers with no major [degree] or certificate in the subject. In the case of math taught in grades five through twelve, the fraction is one-half. Many such students are being taught math by graduates in physical education."[23]

I am not the only one who believes that "certification" is not synonymous with effective teaching. A survey of superintendents and principals, done by Public Agenda, found that only thirteen percent of principals and seven percent of superintendents believe that certification guarantees a typical teacher "has what it takes" to make it in the classroom.[24]

An article in the Society for Quality Education quoted a report by UCLA professor W. James Popham, who demonstrated on three separate occasions that teachers trained in teachers colleges do no better than laymen (housewives, automobile mechanics, and electricians) in promoting student achievement:

> The housewives, electricians and auto mechanics were exactly as effective as the professionally trained, credentialed, experienced teachers.[25]

Teacher preparation, as provided by colleges of education, does not result in increased student achievement. This is supported by teachers themselves when asked about the preparation they received in their school of education:

> About 62 percent of all new teachers—almost two thirds—report they felt unprepared for the realities of their classroom. As former Secretary of Education Arne Duncan has said, "Imagine what our country would do if 62 percent of our doctors felt unprepared to practice medicine—you would have a revolution in our medical schools."[26]

Is it any wonder our children do not do well academically? For a student to become mentally engaged in a subject, the student needs a teacher who is passionate about the subject and who can stimulate his or her intellectual interest and natural curiosity. Teachers without sub-ject-matter mastery simply cannot do that; and we are now living with the results. Today, the United States has the lowest percentage of college students studying math or science of any country in the developed world.[27] As is well known, scientists and engineers are the fuel of any modern economy. If we are serious about STEM (science, technology, engineering, and math) training for our young people, the only way to make that happen, is to ensure we have content-competent teachers instructing our students.

However, the failure to teach our children math and science is not just about scientists and engineers; rather, it is a major failing in the preparation of our children for any scholarly endeavor in which they may choose to engage. Basic skills in math and science are valuable for all citizens to possess, regardless of the career or job they eventually choose. However, as discussed earlier, a well-educated child needs to learn much more than math or science.

Certification laws also discourage competent people from joining the teaching profession because they require everyone, including experienced professionals, to return to college to obtain a teaching degree. That means people who already have had a successful career must become "certified" to do something they may already know how to do. Young people who earned a different degree in college (not in their college's school of education), such as math, biology, or English, cannot work as a teacher in a public school without taking at least another year of college in an approved school of education. Older people, who have had a successful career in another profession, such as the sciences, journalism, or the military, and would like to transfer into teaching, find they have to return to college and get a formal teaching certificate. In some cases, that can require years of additional college and tuition expenses, all to teach a subject a career professional may have already mastered.

For example, no symphony conductor would be allowed to teach music. Bill Gates, without a formal teaching certificate, would not be allowed to teach computer science; no retired astronaut would be allowed to teach math or astronomy. No veteran would be allowed to teach physical education, or a course in leadership. These are extreme examples, perhaps, but they are genuinely illustrative. Throughout the country there are thousands of highly qualified people who would like to teach, perhaps because they would like an exciting change of work, or because they like the idea of helping young people, but they are prevented from doing so because they are not formally "certified."

One evening I was having dinner with a woman who had spent 15 years in the advertising business. She had earned a bachelor's degree and a master of business administration degree, and her position at the time was CEO of an advertising firm. She had done very well in her career and had decided she would like to have a second career. She wanted to become a teacher. She visited one of her state's schools of education and was told she would have to enter as a freshman in order to get her teaching certificate. She decided to stay in advertising—a clear loss for students and for our public schools.

Recent experience with many Teach For America teachers has shown that non-certified instructors can do exemplary work in the classroom. Many of these young graduates, from some of our finest colleges, have achieved amazing results, even with the hardest-to-teach kids. These young people, who evince a passion for teaching, are producing some of the greatest academic gains in some of our lowest-performing schools. They are proving that even children living in the most destitute home conditions can perform at exemplary levels when provided with focused, quality instruction. The Teach For America program shows that the problem with our public schools has little to do with our children's supposed inability to learn, but everything to do with our adults' real ability to teach.

Finding qualified people willing to teach is not the problem, as demonstrated by the experience of The New Teacher Project (TNTP). TNTP is a nonprofit organization that recruits skilled people into the teaching profession. In 2006, TNTP was asked to hire 1,200 teachers to staff low-performing schools for the New York City Public Schools. It received over 8,000 applications. Some the applicants were doctors, lawyers, business people, and researchers. None of the applicants were formally certified under New York State's normal process, but the 1,200 people selected were put through a teacher-training program, managed by the TNTP, and then placed in a public school. Each new teacher was assigned a mentor to assist during the first year of teaching. Regardless of the city in which TNTP is seeking recruits, it receives many more applicants than open positions. Since its founding in 1997, TNTP has placed 37,000 teachers into high-need schools.[28]

Moreover, because of the large applicant pool, TNTP is able to be selective and TNTP leaders can ensure that only highly qualified people enter the classroom. In my view, this is how the entire process of public school hiring should be managed.

Of course, not every school of education is a poor one. I have visited many excellent schools and have become friends with their deans. However, I am talking about a few excellent schools of education, not hundreds. Based upon Dr. Levine's assessment, the vast majority of schools, charged with granting teaching certificates, are not good at their task and have no business preparing professionals to teach our children. These mediocre schools exist to collect tuition and to turn out people with a teaching credential. They do not exist to train teachers who are effective educators. The measure of teacher effectiveness should be the ability to improve student learning (outcomes) and not the number of courses completed at a school of education (inputs).

Recently, I spoke with the dean of one of America's highest-rated education schools. I asked him about how selective he was for admission into his program. He indicated a desire to be far more selective, but said he could not do so and still achieve the revenue budget he was assigned. Basically, without saying it, he was acknowledging the fact that his school was a profit center for his university and it was his responsibility to insure that he achieved his budget. I found it interesting that even one of our best education schools was being compromised by the system.

Schools of education have not shown they can turn out great teachers, and state certification laws have not provided a reliable supply of qualified teachers in the classroom. Both systems need to be changed.

We should either eliminate the notion of certification or modify it dramatically so that teacher certification is something one earns, on the job, after proving that children actually learn effectively under one's instruction. If we must maintain the state requirement of certification, then I recommend that we modify the laws to require a minimum of three years of in-class teaching before one qualifies for certification.

I believe, however, that certification laws should simply be eliminated, and that schools of education should justify their existence by proving that completing their training programs significantly enhances a teacher's ability to teach. Business schools operate exactly this way, and it works.

Ending certification restrictions would yield other benefits as well. First, many poor-quality education schools would close, and those that remained would be in greater demand because they would be able to demonstrate that their course work is beneficial to making their graduates good teachers. Having fewer and better schools of education would make entry into the profession more competitive. One of the fastest ways to enhance the profession of teaching would be to make it more difficult to enter.

Schools and districts need to raise teaching standards, and in response, schools of education need to raise their admission requirements. Eliminating certification laws is the first step to enhancing educational training and to building up the stature of the teaching profession.

An example of this occurred in Finland. Back in the 1980s, the Finnish government determined that "education was the only thing that could save their country from being left behind."[29] The Finns decided that the only way to get serious about education was to select highly educated people, the best and brightest of each generation, and train them rigorously. So, that's what they did.[30] Today, Finland's students are among the highest-performing students in the world and the result is a transformed country.

One of the steps the Finns took was to dismantle their existing education schools. As the U.S. does today, Finland had many small education colleges around the country. Today, it has only a few, located in major universities. Entry into one of these schools is as difficult as getting into a medical school. Only about 10 percent of those who apply are able to get in. Teaching has become a very "high status" profession in Finland.

The same is true for Singapore, which has another high-performing school system. There, to become a teacher, you must have graduated from college, graduated in the top third of your class and majored in the subject you wish to teach. Only if you meet these criteria will you be considered for a position in teaching. Of those who meet these criteria, only one in twelve actually becomes a teacher.[31]

A 2010 study by McKinsey and Company found that 100 percent of new teachers in the best-performing school systems in the world—Finland, Singapore, and South Korea—come from the top third of their college classes. In contrast, 77 percent of new U.S. teachers come from the bottom two-thirds of their college classes.[32]

By having only their brightest people entering the profession, the Finns were able to deregulate their schools and give both principals and

teachers total freedom on how they taught their students. They were able to "dismantle its most oppressive regulations, piece by piece." Further, "The government abolished school inspections. It didn't need them anymore."[33]

As the Finns deregulated their schools, they enhanced the profession of teaching by giving teachers and principals the kind of autonomy that other professionals enjoy.

Also, by reducing the number of education schools and restricting admission, they made education schools become more relevant in the preparation of teachers. Attending one of these schools became a requirement, not because of certification laws, but because they turned out proven teachers.

Another outcome of certification laws, combined with tenure, is that teaching has become a career occupation. This situation results in our children having teachers who have usually spent their entire working lives in the classroom. In some cases that may be desirable, but often these teachers have limited ability to impart many of life's skills that one acquires from having other life experiences. As was pointed out earlier, the mission of a school involves the "total development" of a child. That includes much more than academics. Restricting the profession to teachers who have never had another job, who have never engaged in any other life endeavor, greatly limits their scope of teaching about life. Typically, the most-remembered and best college professors were those with experiences outside of the classroom, who could bring real-life experiences into their daily lessons. We need to bring the same benefit to our public schools. Today, because of certification laws, those types of discussions can be limited in quantity and narrow in scope.

Removing certification laws would also allow tens of thousands of citizens, who have developed skills and wonderful experiences, and who would love to teach children, to get into the profession. Former members of the military, mid-career professionals and retirees from government, nonprofits or business are examples. We do our children a great disser-

vice by preventing these citizens from sharing their knowledge with our children.

Certification laws are the "gatekeeper" of education, and these laws are keeping the most qualified people out of the profession. Eliminating, or substantially modifying, certification laws is the fastest way to correct all of these teaching-quality problems and to enhance the stature of the teaching profession.

## 2. Placement and Working Conditions

HIRING OF new teachers normally occurs in the summer and a new teacher begins teaching in the fall. In the few weeks (sometimes only days) between being hired and the start of the school year, a new teacher is expected to prepare for students. Seldom will a new teacher be given a mentor or extensive teaching materials such as lesson plans, or provided with useful information from the prior teacher who taught in that classroom. Also, a teacher is generally given minimal, if any, information about the learning readiness of her incoming students. Thus, in many cases, a new teacher must "reinvent the wheel" when embarking upon his or her teaching career.

If all these conditions weren't difficult enough, early on-the-job training is often nonexistent, unlike other professions. A new teacher is expected to know, at the outset, what to do and how to do it. Some do, and some don't. New teachers are generally given the most difficult students to teach in the most resource-poor schools. This occurs because experienced teachers use seniority to choose both the schools where they work and the students they will teach. In no other profession would the newest hires be given the most difficult assignments. Such mismatched work assignments would not even be considered, let alone tolerated, in other fields.

Some new teachers are lucky to begin work at a school with an outstanding principal. When that occurs, new teachers have someone to help them adjust to new surroundings and to offer assistance. When that help is not there, and often it is not, new teachers are still expected to perform at a high level.

Unlike the case in other professions, the "best practices" learned in teaching are seldom shared, even within a school building, let alone across a whole district. The reason is that all teachers are scheduled to be in class with students at the same time, which hinders a new teacher from observing or being mentored by an experienced educator. Also, teachers are teaching all the school day, so there are limited opportunities to observe or discuss teaching strategies with peers.

Working conditions in many schools are also appalling. In some cases the buildings are old and poorly maintained: bathrooms don't always work, paint is chipping off walls, hallways are cluttered, graffiti remains on the walls, etc. In many cases, there aren't enough textbooks or supplies. I could go on, but it suffices to say that some of our teachers face many other problems than just poorly prepared students.

Teachers just entering the profession need to be treated the way starting doctors and engineers are treated. They need to work initially with experts to hone their skills. A doctor does not come out of medical school ready to perform major surgery. That skill is learned over several years while being guided by a skilled surgeon. The same is true for engineers. A new engineer is considered an apprentice until passing a licensing exam and obtaining a good deal of on-the-job training under the tutelage of an experienced engineer. In no case is a newly trained doctor or engineer given the most difficult patient or project right from the start.

Another aspect of teaching that restricts a teacher's ability to succeed is the regimented school day and the lack of time teachers have to prepare for their students.

Betty Wallace and William Graves described a teacher's life in *The Poisoned Apple*:

Anyone who has taught in public schools will understand why teachers rely on textbooks. They are daily expected to deliver at least five, sometimes more, forty-five minute lessons. Typically, they have at most one period a day to prepare. It is as impossible for a teacher to prepare five interesting presentations a day, as it would be for a pastor to prepare five daily sermons or for a politician to develop a new speech for every campaign stop.[34]

William Stevenson and James Stigler relate a Chinese reaction to this situation:

When we informed the Chinese teachers that American elementary school teachers are responsible for their classes all day long, they looked incredulous. How could any teacher be expected to do a good job when there is not time outside of class to prepare and correct lessons, work with individual children, consult with other teachers and attend to all the matters that arise in a typical day at school?[35]

Focus group discussions with teachers, all over the country, have shown that job satisfaction is the biggest problem facing teachers. Surveys measuring job satisfaction show that lack of support and not being treated with respect rank above compensation in importance.[36] This is not surprising, since those entering the profession know, in advance, what their compensation will be. It is also not surprising that teachers constantly push to receive more money, because they do not have control over other factors that promote respect and job satisfaction. If you don't like your working conditions, it is normal to complain that you do not make enough money.

If teachers could enter the profession with ongoing support to help them be successful in the classroom, many young teachers would remain in the profession, even with the compensation they now receive. Frustration with their inability to be successful, that is, to see that children learn under their tutelage, drives many teachers to pursue other vocations. Fixing this aspect of the teaching profession would dramatically reduce turnover, improve student achievement, and greatly increase teacher job satisfaction, even if we didn't significantly boost compensation.

## 3. Compensation

TEACHERS' COMPENSATION comes in two types: base compensation, which is the pay that all teachers receive, and incentive compensation, which results from additional training or on-the-job performance.

### Base Compensation

Almost everyone, including legislators, agree that teachers do not make enough money. Teaching is a skilled occupation, yet many people in the profession can hardly afford to pay the rent. Teachers working in urban and affluent suburban school systems claim they often cannot afford to live in the district where they work. Many in the profession believe they are overworked, under-appreciated, and underpaid.

Most teachers will tell you they work many more hours than the length of the workday for which they are paid. Good teachers will spend two to three hours a night correcting papers and preparing for the next day's classes. Moreover, teachers attend classes during the summer and on school days arrive early to get ready for students. None of this time is compensated. This, of course, is not unique to teaching. Most professions have people who often work evenings and weekends, if needed, without additional compensation. Also, not all teachers work after hours and over the summer. The dedicated teachers do, and they are definitely underpaid.

In almost all states, teacher pay is driven by a salary schedule depending on years of service and academic credits obtained. Nothing in the compensation system rewards teaching excellence. This type of structured compensation system was installed in the 1920s "to ensure equal treatment for all."[37]

Over the intervening 98 years our entire society has changed, but the compensation system for teachers has remained largely the same, except that the dollar amounts in the schedule have dramatically increased. The current compensation system rewards mediocrity at the same rate as excellence. No other profession operates this way. The current teacher compensation system is broken and needs to be totally changed.

Though teachers do not earn as much money as people in some other professions, if you look carefully, you will find the problem of teacher pay is not a matter of compensation at all. It is a matter of employment. **Teachers are not underpaid or underworked, they are underemployed.**

That is perhaps a radical statement, but the hourly compensation of teachers is really quite competitive with other professions. The average teacher in most states is paid a very attractive hourly wage. For example, average teacher pay in Seattle is $77,239 for a ten-month work year.[38] That is low for the annual compensation of a trained professional. However, that same teacher is actually making $58.51 an hour, plus a generous package of benefits that few private-sector employers can match. Teachers in Seattle are employed for 1,320 hours per year, regardless of how many hours they might actually work. If that teacher were employed for a standard year of 2,080 hours, at the same hourly rate, their annual salary would be $121,710, a very competitive salary for a college graduate. Bear in mind, this comparison is based on the average salary. Thus, some teachers are making substantially more than that amount, while new teachers make less.

The above numbers are based upon an urban system (Seattle). Some states are paying more than that and some less. The highest average pay for a teacher is in the state of New York, where teachers average $79,637 statewide.[39] South Dakota has the lowest average compensation at $42,688.[40] Those differences reflect the substantial difference in cost of living between those two states. Using the same 2080-hour year, these equate to $125,488 and $67,266, respectively, plus a benefit package that is well above that found in major corporations.

Looking at the above analysis, it becomes obvious that what we have is an employment problem, not a compensation problem. The way for teachers to make more money is to employ them for more hours in the year. One quick move would be to employ teachers for eight hours a day. Today, a Seattle elementary teacher is employed for seven hours a day and a secondary teacher for seven-and-a-half hours a day. Just employing them for the standard eight hours would generate a seven to fourteen percent increase in compensation, and would begin to close the gap between the hours compensated and the actual number of hours worked. It would also allow principals more time with teachers for staff meetings, evaluation meetings, student assessment, and curriculum planning. Additionally, it would allow teachers more time to spend with students and other teachers during and after the school day.

Further, it is obvious that as our schools move to create standards-based learning environments, some children will need to attend class for more hours per day and more days per year in order to achieve the academic standard. Not all children can and do learn the same amount of information in the same amount of time. This means that, to ensure the effective education of all children, some children will need a longer day and a longer year. Some schools will need to stay open longer and that means some teachers will be employed for more hours. (See Chapter 9 for more information on this issue.)

This evolving situation presents both a requirement and an opportunity. Currently, all teachers are employed for the 180-day school year, even though they are paid a fixed amount per month. Erroneously, teacher compensation is often considered as an annual salary when, in reality, it is a ten-month salary. In fact, it is even less than a ten-month salary because teachers are employed only seven hours per day and school is not in session every work day during those ten months.

It is obvious, however, that some people go into teaching because they like having summers off and because it allows them to be home when their children are home. This is not something that is likely to change, nor need it change for all teachers.

Recognizing that fact suggests we should think about hiring teachers under different annual contracts. For example, teachers could choose to work for nine months, ten months or eleven months. Those choosing the ten- or eleven-month contracts would make substantially more money, but they obviously wouldn't get summers off. Those teachers could work with students who need more learning time before moving to the next level, or as mentors for new teachers before the start of a new school year. Teachers would indicate their desired contract year and district officials would decide which teachers to hire under each type of contract.

Another option would be to increase the length of the school year to be more similar to other developed nations. Moving to a 200-day school year would give teachers an immediate 11% raise.

## Incentive Compensation

Longer-year contracts would create a way for teachers to receive a professional level of compensation, but longer contracts would not solve the problem of incentive. Even under longer contracts, mediocre teachers could receive as much or more money than excellent teachers.

The current system allows a teacher to make more money only by accumulating seniority or earning more credits and degrees from a school of education. Neither criterion gives any indication of whether the teacher has improved his or her instructional skill or is more effective in helping children learn. Thus, a very poor teacher with 20 years of experience will earn more than an excellent teacher with five years of experience. No other profession works this way.

To rectify this, I recommend the establishment of "career ladders" for the profession. This would allow excellence to be rewarded by making a promotion ladder available to teachers who excel.

Teachers should be paid based on their ability, not on their years of service. Teaching talent can be measured by the learning that occurs in the classroom. Teachers whose students learn under their tutelage should make more money than teachers who fail to educate children effectively. In fact, an ineffective teacher should not be allowed to remain in the classroom, wasting students' learning time.

With a career ladder, a good teacher has access to a future of increasing compensation based on performance. A career ladder would include job titles corresponding to levels such as Apprentice Teacher, Teacher, Senior Teacher and Master Teacher. A teacher would be promoted to the next level only after a certain number of years and a series of positive evaluations. Such a program would reward performance, and would give teachers the opportunity to increase their income while remaining in the profession. Teachers who did not get promoted beyond an apprentice level after a few years would be invited to leave the profession.

You will note that I have not recommended a bonus system, often referred to as "merit pay." These differ from the promotion ladder idea because a bonus is a one-year compensation increase versus a permanent increase in pay. Bonuses, paid to only a few people, can often be disruptive to the organization. Though many people promote the notion of merit pay, I have come to the conclusion that it is not a good idea.

I once studied the functioning of a school district that had implemented merit pay. The outcome was not what had been intended. Teachers who received the merit pay were unwilling to share their teaching expertise for fear of not getting a merit bonus the following year (there was a limited amount of bonus funds available). Teachers who failed to get merit pay tended to ostracize those who did. Both responses were detrimental to the academic effectiveness of a school.

Another reason individual merit pay is not practical in public schools is that each teacher is very dependent on the teacher who taught the students in the prior year. For example, the "internal customer" of a first-grade teacher is the second-grade teacher. If the first-grade teacher fails to prepare the students, then the second-grade teacher's ability to advance student learning will suffer, even if the second-grade teacher is truly outstanding. This is why a merit pay system can be looked upon as being unfair. All members of the faculty must carry their weight if all students are to achieve. If one teacher fails to do the job properly, the next teacher in line is hindered in his or her work. Each teacher must strive to deliver to the next teacher students who have achieved their learning goals for that grade level.

If we want to incentivize teachers beyond the career ladder mentioned above, then I would favor "whole school" bonuses rather than individual merit pay. Providing a bonus opportunity for the entire faculty would give every teacher a strong financial incentive and provide built-in pressure for every teacher to perform.

## Conclusion

IF WE are serious about educating all of our children, we must alter the ways we select, train, and compensate our teachers. Improving the selection and training of teachers would not cost extra money; in fact, it may well be done with less money, with substantially improved results. The ideas presented here that involve compensation will require more money. However, every state is already spending a lot of money in dealing with high turnover and having to hire and train new teachers to replace those who leave the profession. Those costs are never accounted for, but they are substantial, not only in dollars, but in reduced student achievement.

Providing students with access to gifted teachers during a longer day and a longer year would create a good chance of keeping kids in school through graduation, ready to secure good jobs or more education. This would reduce the costs we now spend on the juvenile justice system and on the social services provided by the federal and state governments. Universities and community colleges would also save money by not having to provide extensive remedial courses. Further, better-educated students would yield increased tax revenues, as these students graduate and become productive, tax-paying citizens. Finally, students who remain in school increase the revenue to the school and district that would have been lost if the students dropped out.

With the exception of eliminating certification laws, none of these ideas need be implemented immediately. They could be phased in over several years. Increasing the number of hours teachers are employed could be adopted as gradually as the state could afford. Every hour added would make the profession more attractive and would reduce turnover. Adding experienced mentors would also be a great addition to improving teacher job satisfaction.

All of the above commentary pertains to modifications to the existing method of compensation, i.e., a state salary schedule. Another way to address the compensation of teachers is to eliminate the state salary schedule completely and let individual districts and individual schools decide on the compensation for teachers. In this scenario, teachers would be hired by either the district or the school, and would be paid what was needed to hire and retain them, much as all businesses operate. This would only work if we totally retrain both principals and superintendents to understand how to hire staff in conjunction with the availability of funds from their own budget. This is not done in public schools, but it is the way both private schools and charter schools operate. It would require public schools to be free of the typical union contract terms. Also, under this system, employee benefits, like medical insurance and pensions, would likely continue to be managed at the district level.

Today, there are thousands of wonderfully qualified people in the teaching profession. They remain in the profession in spite of the obstacles described in this chapter. We owe it to them, and to those who will follow, to treat them and compensate them like the professionals they are. Teaching is perhaps our most vital profession, but we are not devoting the time or money required to make the profession all it needs to be. By not doing so, we have discouraged our best and brightest people from entering the teaching profession and we have deprived our children of the teachers they both need and deserve.

# 6. Leadership

WHY IS IT SOME SCHOOLS PROPEL EVERY CHILD TO REACH HIGH achievement levels and others do not—sometimes even among schools in the same district? Why is it some schools have very few disruptions by students, while others, with similar student populations, have constant discipline problems? Why is it some schools have virtually no staff turnover and others have a revolving door of staff? Why is it some schools have very high student and staff attendance rates and other schools do not? The answer to each of these questions rests with the quality of leadership present in the building.

High-performing schools share many characteristics, but none is more important than leadership. *A visionary principal always leads an effective school.* In fact, it is impossible for a school to become effective without the leadership of a visionary leader who is able to rally the support and commitment of the entire faculty and parent community, regardless of the makeup of the student body. The same is true for a school district.

Some people who are frustrated with the quality of public education believe it can be improved only by the use of charters, vouchers, or both. However, even at a charter school or under a voucher system, effective leadership is the primary driver of success.

As with any organization, the impact of effective leadership on a school's performance is profound. A study by Branch, Hanushek, and Rivkin found that "a highly effective principal raises student achievement from two to seven additional months of learning in a single school year."[1] A study in 2004, funded by the Wallace Foundation, found that 25 percent of student achievement can be traced to the school leader.[2] Can you imagine what our schools would be like if they were all led by effective principals?

Unfortunately, public education is virtually devoid of effective leadership. I say this knowing full well that we have some absolutely amazing schools operating inside public education. However, these schools number in the hundreds, at best a thousand or so, among almost 100,000 schools nationwide. We also do not have a single major district that can be considered highly effective in educating all students. If we had effective leadership throughout the system, that would not be the case. Effective leaders would not tolerate the performance level of today's schools.

So why is public education nearly devoid of effective leaders? We addressed this issue in Chapter 1, by pointing out that the present system develops education leader not upon who has proven leadership ability, but upon who wants to be an education administrator. Leadership development in public education is a process-driven system, not a competency-driven system. Further, the quality of leadership training provided is at best mediocre.

Richard Elmore, a professor of educational leadership at Harvard, says it this way:

> [T]he vast majority of people who are certified as educational leaders still come from largely part-time, cash-for-credit certification programs in small institutions, operating under traditional state-certification requirements, without significant research capacity, and staffed heavily by part-time faculty members.[3]

Moreover, in most states, there are numerous institutions licensed to grant teacher and principal certificates. A person could be a terrible teacher and still be accepted into one of these principal training programs. Acceptance virtually assures graduation, and graduation virtually ensures employment, because we have a shortage of principals. Furthermore, once hired, one is assured of gaining tenure. Each step leads invariably to the next, and tenure provides functional lifetime employment for even the most incompetent leaders. Elmore goes on to say:

> And despite the existence of the ISLC (Interstate School Leaders Licensure Consortium) standards, empirical evidence on the state of

curriculum and teaching in leadership-preparation programs paints a picture of relatively low-level content that is disconnected from mainstream research and practice in public and private organizations outside the education sector. The existence of alternative programs and providers has not broken the traditional cartel of higher education institutions, state departments of education, and local districts that has controlled leadership preparation for a century or more.[4]

This method of training, hiring, and promoting leaders is unique to public education, which is the only professional segment of our society in which *promotion is based upon self-selection*. Almost any teacher can decide to become a principal, and, once the decision has been made, can achieve that goal. All a teacher has to do is leave the classroom for a year and attend an education college for the required courses to obtain a principal certification. In fact, it has been shown that our worst teachers are often the first to apply to become principals. A common refrain is: "If you can't make it in the classroom, become an administrator."

As was pointed out earlier, this same procedure is followed for choosing superintendents. In most states, superintendents must also be certified. The state's education colleges also grant this credential. Education training programs, particularly for superintendents, are faulty in both their entry requirements and their curricula. Many of the skills required to be a good superintendent, particularly for an urban school district, are not taught in schools of education. Consequently, most superintendents come out of these programs poorly equipped for the job and, in most cases, lacking in leadership talent as well.

The whole system of promotion and leadership development in public education is broken. The most effective principals and superintendents report they became effective leaders "in spite of the system, not because of it."

As was the case for teachers, the source of this problem is certification laws. These laws again give a monopoly to education schools for the development of education leaders. Frankly, the last place on any college campus that I would look for leaders would be the education school, but that is the only place our schools can look. Unless and until we change this, our education system will continue to be devoid of effective leadership and will continue to fail in the task of effectively educating all students.

Strong leaders will enable improvements for the system as a whole, regardless of any lesser decisions a government or school district makes. Effective educational leaders will not tolerate the system we have now; they will find a way to change it, one way or another.

Two examples of this point can be seen in the actions of Rod Paige, former superintendent of Houston Public Schools who later became the U.S. Secretary of Education, and John Stanford, the former major general who became superintendent of Seattle Public Schools. Both men were leaders; one was a formally trained educator and one was not.

Rod Paige was a teacher, a football coach, a college professor, and a dean of a school of education before becoming superintendent of the Houston Public Schools. His background training and innate talents made him an effective education leader. During his tenure, Houston made great strides in decentralizing decision-making and in improving academic achievement for all students. Paige's leadership skills were developed over time, as he took on new and increasingly challenging positions. By the time he became a superintendent, he not only had the skills needed for the job, but had the knowledge of what was needed to fix a major urban public education system. Houston, under Paige's leadership, was touted nationally as one of the premier examples of an urban school district on the mend.

John Stanford served thirty years in the U.S. Army. He once told me that ten of those thirty years were spent in some type of training. Stanford attended Pennsylvania State University for his bachelor's degree and received a master's degree in public policy from Michigan State University. He also attended the Army War College and completed numerous leadership-training courses during his time in the Army. Throughout his military career, he held a variety of leadership positions, including leading troops in combat. Upon retiring from the military, General Stanford was appointed county executive of Fulton County, Georgia (the county that includes Atlanta). In less than four years General Stanford was able to completely restructure county government, install over $1 billion of infrastructure improvements, put the county's financial house in order, and do it all without raising taxes.

By the time General Stanford became superintendent of Seattle Public Schools, he had honed his leadership skills to a very fine level. In his two-and-a-half years as superintendent, he not only transformed Seattle Public Schools but transformed the attitude of an entire city toward its public school system, achieving widespread support. He eliminated mandatory busing, decentralized decision-making, installed a new funding policy, and negotiated a union contract that eliminated seniority in the hiring of teachers. He became gravely ill during the last six months of his tenure and, sadly, died of leukemia 38 months after becoming superintendent.

Both individuals, and their accomplishments, are classic examples of the power of effective leadership. Effective leaders can create a movement, even in an entrenched bureaucracy. However, that is unlikely to happen in our education system, as we have so few effective leaders and the current leadership training system is unlikely to change that. In addition, those leaders outside the system who would like to bring their skills to education are unable to do so because they cannot get in.

One way to develop effective leadership is to overhaul the method of promotion. Businesses and the military have promotion processes in place that the education community could emulate. In the business world, promotion occurs on the basis of evaluation and proven performance. Generally, when a person is promoted, he or she is given additional training either inside or outside the company, but in either case paid for by the company. Sometimes, companies will even send outstanding employees back to college. Many companies will gladly pay for some or all of the cost of a master of business administration (MBA) program for their most valued employees. Large companies such as General Electric, IBM, Microsoft, and Motorola have their own advanced training centers for employees, where they invest heavily in cultivating leaders for a future role in their respective organizations.

MBA programs, at most universities, have stringent entrance requirements. Only the best and brightest are admitted. Typically, students have already distinguished themselves in some field and have survived a rigorous screening process. Thus, MBA applicants have already demonstrated leadership talent before they enter the program. Graduates of these programs either return to their employer, if the employer sent them to school or contributed to tuition, or obtain a junior-level management position with a company. In both cases, an individual is not promoted until he or she has proven an ability to perform in a leadership position. Some students leave the programs and start their own businesses.

The military operates in a similar way. Promotions are based upon performance evaluations. Additionally, many officers graduate from a military academy that has very competitive entrance requirements and that admits only the most outstanding applicants. Graduates leave the academies as second lieutenants or ensigns and start up the ladder of promotion based upon performance.

If public education selected, trained, and promoted talented employees in this fashion, schools would quickly improve, because only the best candidates would become principals. Thus, only those properly prepared would be placed in a leadership position. The same would be true of superintendents.

Public education is a government institution, so proposed changes may correlate better with the military illustration rather than with the business one. For example, the federal government fully funds four major universities (the military academies) for the sole purpose of training leaders for our military. These four institutions provide each branch of the military with a constant supply of well-trained, carefully selected leaders who have the capacity to maintain our country's military readiness and defend our nation.

There is no similar leadership training for public education. There is not even one institution, fully funded by federal, state, or local governments, established to train leaders for our schools. It is time we founded a West Point for education—though I would suggest a two-year school, rather than West Point's four-year undergraduate model. The graduate school would operate much like advanced business schools and be funded like the military academies. Such an institution or institutions would accept only outstanding candidates who were certain of their desire to be an educational leader, passed a rigorous application process, and showed meaningful leadership skills in their early professional work. These schools could also operate on an "invitation only" basis. Individuals would have to be invited to attend such schools. This is the way Singapore trains its leaders. They all come from the teaching corps and are all "invited" to become principals. Only outstanding teachers, who have shown leadership qualities, are invited.

Educators graduating from such a school, or schools, could receive a master of education administration (MEA) or similar degree and would be hired as vice principals in large schools, or perhaps directly as principals in small schools.

Fully funded by the government, these schools could be separate institutions, or simply be leadership academies created on college campuses. Students would accept government-funded tuition and board in exchange for a four-year commitment to the field of public education. If the education-leadership academy was integrated into a university program, then the government funding could funnel to students differently, such as through scholarship awards, with the same four-year commitment to the field of public education required.

If the federal government was unwilling to set up such institutions, then states could act. In fact, we need multiple schools for this purpose, so it might be more practical and make more sense to have states take on this assignment. As I indicated, these schools could become part of an existing state university, but could also be independent. Being associated with, but not part of, a university might allow for more flexibility in operations and in staffing.

Such a school or schools would offer an interdisciplinary curriculum, including courses in subjects relevant to the job of principal and superintendent. Professors from education, business, public policy, and even medicine could be employed. Also, sitting principals and superintendents could be employed to teach specific classes. Students would be exposed to problems likely to be faced by an education leader. Issues such as employee evaluations, hiring, labor relations, finance and budgeting, public relations and media, and influencing politicians would all be covered, in addition to basic courses in curriculum planning and effective teaching. Students would also spend extensive time shadowing principals or superintendents in order to get first-hand experience of the position. Would-be superintendents would also get training in construction management, bonding, marketing bonds and levies, union negotiations, etc. Graduates would be well-prepared and capable of becoming agents of change in their new positions.

An example of one such program has been established at the University of Virginia. For the 2013–14 school year, the faculty of the Darden School (business) and the faculty of the Curry School (education) developed a unique dual MBA/MEd degree. Students begin at Curry during the first summer and then take traditional business courses at the Darden School during their first year. In their second summer, students take courses at Curry and can participate in an internship. In their second year, students take courses in both schools. Students admitted to this program have gone through the same admission process required of traditional Darden students.

Though it was assumed that the students entering the program would be interested in becoming education leaders such as principals and superintendents, the reality is that some students have even broader interests. Some want to go into consulting with a special focus on education, while others want to start new charter schools or found education technology startups. Some are even interested in finance jobs that involve providing capital for new ventures or investing in public-for-profit companies that serve education.

Regardless of where these graduates end up, the program will turn out well-trained leaders with a passion for education. That can only be good for our schools. It will be interesting to see whether this program can achieve its lofty goals and whether it will be replicated elsewhere.

In addition to the creation of education leadership academies, we must also develop programs to enhance the skills of current superintendents and principals. Such programs would be similar to the executive management programs offered by many business schools. These would be one- to six-week residential programs in which superintendents and principals would take courses designed to enhance their skills for their respective administrative positions. School districts and charitable foundations, along with state and federal governments, would fund these programs. Most major universities could create these short-term, intensive, focused programs in concert with their education and business schools.

After discussing this idea in 2001 with then-Dean Kim Clark of the Harvard Business School (HBS), I was pleased to see that school engaged in furthering this exact model. HBS has partnered with the Harvard Graduate School of Education (HGSE) and has developed a program for superintendents and their immediate staff. The program is called the Public Education Leadership Project (PELP). The program started in 2003 and so far 29 school districts have participated in PELP with positive results. Arne Duncan, the former U.S. Secretary of Education, was a graduate of PELP. HBS has also published a book written by HBS and HGSE faculty covering case studies of various school districts and the issues they face. Over 45,000 copies have been sold and are now being used throughout the country.

The University of Virginia started a similar executive-management program composed of faculty members from the Darden School of Business and the Curry School of Education. This is in addition to the degree program mentioned above. Whereas the Harvard program trains superintendents and a school district's top seven managers, the Virginia program started by offering advanced training for 40 education leaders from two districts in Florida. Those 40 people included the superintendents and some management personnel, plus members of the community. Both programs started in 2003 and have received rave reviews from attendees. Since starting this effort, the Curry and Darden schools have worked with 75 districts from 15 states on improving district operations and on teaching principals and district leaders how to work together to turn around failing schools.

Charter schools are also working on leadership development. Their program is much more aligned with what is done in industry. Teachers, who are already carefully selected, are constantly assessed for their leadership skills and their willingness to take on leadership roles. Selected teachers are then given leadership assignments within their building. Assuming they perform those assignments satisfactorily, they are then selected to go into a principal-training program that will include extensive internships in schools led by outstanding principals. Upon graduation, they are given vice principal assignments. All schools have at least one vice principal, and in all of them the job of principal includes being a mentor to aspiring principals. Both the Knowledge Is Power Program (KIPP) and Summit Charter schools have programs similar to this. In both cases, they have decided to "grow their own," as they seldom can find acceptable candidates within the public system.

## Conclusion

AMERICA'S PUBLIC education system needs to be transformed. Educational success for children will require superb leadership at all levels. Developing a system of selecting and training effective leaders is a necessary step to achieving that success. Such a system must be a top priority of federal and state education policy.

To begin this process, states need to eliminate certification laws. These laws have failed in their purpose and are now a major constraint in improving our schools. Without these laws, education schools would have to improve to retain their existence, and other schools on a university campus could be employed in preparing both our teachers and our leaders for a future in education. In addition, without these laws, more people like John Stanford could be recruited into our education system, to the benefit of all our children.

Principal and superintendent training academies should be established in several locations around the country. These academies should be multidisciplinary institutions that set high and rigid standards for admission and for graduation, and turn out truly gifted leaders who have a passion for education.

The Harvard Business School accepts about 900 students per year, which means that in ten years almost 9,000 people will have graduated with advanced business training. There are slightly more than 14,000 school districts in this country. However, half of America's children attend school in just 800 districts. If, ten years from now, schools and districts had even a few thousand well-trained leaders, we would have an entirely new educational system in this country.

Improving our schools is dependent upon improving the leadership in those schools. To make that happen, we must dramatically change the way we select and train education leaders.

# 7. Governance

Leadership for any organization starts at the top, and for public school districts that means the school board. In most cases, the citizens of a community elect school board members, just as they elect a local mayor and city council members. Local control has been a core principle in public education governance since the inception of the common school, and locally elected school boards are perceived to be a key element to that control.

There are 13,588 school districts in the United States, and a school board leads each district.[1] The number of districts, and therefore the number of school boards in a state, varies considerably, ranging from 17 in Nevada to 1,043 in Texas. My state of Washington has 295 school districts. Boards vary in size, but most have five members. Large urban systems or county-wide districts will often have seven to nine members. Districts vary in size from the smallest, with a few students, to New York City, our country's largest district, with over 1,000,000 students.

The length of a school board term is normally four years. To ensure continuity, the terms are usually sequenced so that a majority of board members' terms expire one year and the remaining members' terms expire two years later. This cycle of elections can cause a school board's entire membership to change in only four years.

Two or more candidates may run for each school board position. Thus, there are a lot of people running for office across each state, proposing a lot of different education agendas.

For most of the past century, board positions were filled by competent, caring people who ran for the school board as part of their civic duty. With small school systems and highly qualified people on the board, there existed strong governance. Today, that strong governance model still works well in some suburban and rural public school systems. However, in urban systems and even some larger suburban school districts, that is no longer the case. Some 800 districts have student populations in excess of 10,000, and these districts enroll slightly more than half of the nation's 50 million students.[2]

Being a board member of one of these larger districts is a much different job than being a board member in a small, rural district. In the larger districts, there can be hundreds of schools and dozens of neighborhoods involved. Candidates are not necessarily from the local neighborhood and are not necessarily a good fit for the office they seek. Candidates for school board are often poorly qualified, and sometimes their service is very detrimental to the effective management of the school system they oversee.

Often they do not understand the level of authority they have. School boards are policy-making bodies, not legislative or operational bodies. Thus, there are a limited number of areas in which boards should be involved. However, many board members do not understand their policy-making function, or they choose to ignore it and then interfere with management and district operations. They become log rollers for petty interests. Again, far from helping, a school board made up of such members can be actively detrimental to the effective operation of a school district.

The decline in the quality and competency of school board candidates is a direct result of several important social changes that have occurred over the past half-century, many of which were enumerated in Chapter 2. During that time, cities lost many qualified people simply because they moved out of the city. Other potential candidates have refused to run because of the increasing personal and financial disclosures required of those running for public office. They simply do not want their entire lives thrown into the public spotlight. Some people choose not to run because of the large number of meetings one has to attend during the campaign, the sheer number of people one has to solicit for support, and the sharply negative personal assaults one must endure from opponents and opponents' supporters.

Still others, because urban systems are media centers and public officials are under constant press scrutiny, find the very public nature of being an elected official unattractive. Public and press scrutiny, and the demands from constituents of varying and often narrow viewpoints, are all common reasons why some people reject running for public office, particularly the school board.

Ironically, public and media attention can often discourage qualified candidates, but tends to attract less desirable candidates to run for office. Such people have not earned enough money to worry about financial disclosure laws, and they enjoy basking in media attention because they have not received much recognition elsewhere in their lives. For them, running for school board provides a wonderful venue for gaining the public exposure they desire. They see it as a way to advance their own agendas and help them possibly move on to higher office, which in turn further enhances their public standing. Neither of these personal ambitions is helpful to the education of our children or to the effective management of a large public education system.

Others may run for school board because they have a specific agenda they want to pursue. They may run because they don't like the superintendent, or don't want a particular school closed, or support or oppose charter schools, a particular curriculum, or any number of other school policies. When I ran for office, one of the other candidates was running to eliminate soda vending machines in the schools. That was her primary policy goal, if elected. Removing soda vending machines from schools was not necessarily a bad idea, but being a single-issue activist did not necessarily qualify her for a position on the school board.

When asked to review candidates for school board in my own city, I have found that they can usually be sorted into one of three categories: social activists, single-issue advocates, and union loyalists. There is nothing wrong with any of these types of people, but they are not the best-qualified people to govern our schools. Their membership on a school board also makes for a volatile mixture of special interests. They have trouble agreeing on a common strategy, and often they simply don't like one another.

Public school systems, particularly those in urban areas, are large, complex organizations. They need wonderfully qualified people who have the competency to plan strategically, to hire effective leaders, and to set policy. In most cases, the people who now run for school board, particularly in urban areas, do not possess those skills.

In early 2005, I asked two leading figures in education (who, be-cause of their respective positions, traveled extensively to urban school systems throughout the country) whether they could name one urban school district that had an effectively operating school board. They both shook their heads and said, "No!" They both found that the problem of unqualified people serving on school boards was pervasive. Now that might have just been the situation at that time, but my own research sug-gests that well-functioning school boards are rare, and, even when they do exist, they do not last.

Effective leadership, and, therefore governance, at the school board level, has nearly become impossible in urban public school systems. Un-qualified people cannot develop effective long-term plans for the im-provement of schools. Qualified people, when they do bravely run and get elected, cannot install any sustainable changes, because within two years (i.e., by the next election), their new colleagues may not agree on the direction the previous board took and may work to develop a new direction. This situation occurs in nearly every large city, and, as a con-sequence, it has prevented long-term sustainable change. Thus, our larg-est public school systems continually perform at substandard levels, or, perhaps more accurately, they tend to perform as they have always per-formed—poorly.

The constant upheaval of school board membership, combined with the fact that usually some members are poorly qualified or unqualified, creates massive turnover in superintendents. Quite often the school district's overarching strategy is the plan of the superintendent and has been endorsed by the current school board. However, if the board's makeup changes, the new members may not want to follow the current plan. Since the plan was likely developed by the existing superintendent, the new members will aim toward hiring a new superintendent. This rapid turnover scenario occurs with great regularity. It has become so bad that the Council of Great City Schools (an organization representing the nation's largest school districts) reports that urban superintendents have an average tenure of only 3.64 years.[3] (This is up from 2.33 years in 1999.[4]) This statistic suggests that every year, over 200 urban districts are searching for a new superintendent.

It is nearly impossible for anyone to make major changes in a large organization in just two or three years. A leader can get started, but that is insufficient time to make a large organization into a more effectively functioning enterprise. Even if a leader can be effective in a short time, as was the case in Seattle, the progress is short-lived. Changing priorities of school boards cause systems to jump from one plan to another, with the ultimate outcome being no meaningful change at all.

Moreover, as was pointed out earlier, there are generally few competent superintendent candidates for boards to evaluate. Thus, a superintendent who has been fired from one school district will often end up being hired by another district. This parade of mediocrity continues until retirement.

Incompetent school board members and a revolving door of superintendents is a recipe for disaster. That is exactly what we have in most urban public school systems, and will continue to have until we either change the manner by which school boards are selected or change the governance model for school districts.

Because of the problems described above, some cities have replaced elected school boards with appointed boards. In most cases, this has occurred when the state legislature has taken over an urban system. The cause of such a takeover is the conclusion by the legislature that the city's schools are beyond repair and unlikely to improve under the existing governance model. Generally, when this occurs, the mayor is given control over the schools and over the selection of the school board. This has been the case in Cleveland, Boston, New York City, Washington, DC, Chicago, and Baltimore. In some cases, the mayor has also selected the superintendent.

This trend toward appointed school boards is an appropriate change in the governance of urban public education systems. Though it is too early to tell whether appointed school boards are better able to institute sustainable change, it is obvious that such a process is likely to yield more qualified board members than the present elected system. If a city has an outstanding mayor, he or she is likely to appoint outstanding school board members. Even a very poor mayor is unlikely to appoint incompetent people to the local school board. Mayors, after all, are more visible to the public—and more accountable.

An even more radical idea would be to eliminate urban school boards entirely. Under this concept, the superintendent would be part of the mayor's cabinet, just like the heads of city departments. The superintendent would be accountable to the mayor. A truly gifted superintendent, leading without a school board, could create a school district governance structure that was effective, efficient, and responsive both to the community and to the teaching staff of the public schools. Though this at first sounds as if it would eliminate local control, it might do just the opposite. A well-run school system would be a great asset to any city. Excellent schools attract families and businesses, and both help make cities more livable for everyone. Most mayors understand this and would work hard to ensure their city had a well-managed and well-functioning school system. The one caveat to this idea is that it requires that the mayor have available a selection of outstanding leaders for the superintendent position. Unfortunately, we don't have that situation now, but could have if the recommendations of Chapter 6 were implemented.

As an example of an effective school system with appointed leadership, look to the universities. With few exceptions, all major public universities have appointed trustees or regents. These appointees are carefully selected and bring a lifetime of relevant experience to their positions. My alma mater is the University of Washington in Seattle. The state governor appoints the regents for this university. Becoming a regent is a great honor, and only the most successful and outstanding citizens are appointed to the position. I cannot imagine how the University of Washington would have achieved its present world-class status if its regents had been popularly elected.

Unless and until qualified candidates choose to run for school board positions (particularly in urban school systems), our students will be better served by an appointed board or no board at all. To improve the quality of urban educational systems, all major cities should at least move to the appointed form of school governance. This would require a change in state law, enabled by a shared outlook of both the legislature and the governor. It would take political courage, which is in short supply these days, but it is nonetheless the right thing to do.

The education of our children is too important to leave to amateurs, local activists, and political junkies. If school boards are retained, then we need to have the best and brightest people serving on them. Improving public education requires an improved governance model, one free of the weaknesses described above. Eliminating the elected school board, particularly for urban school systems, is an idea worth trying, since the present form of governance is clearly not working.

# PART THREE:
# NEXT STEPS

# 8. GROUP VERSUS INDIVIDUALIZED LEARNING

A PARENT NEEDS TO HAVE ONLY TWO CHILDREN TO KNOW HOW TO-tally different children can be. However, America's educational system is set up to educate groups of students rather than each student. The assumption is that group-based learning can be both effective and economical. The results dispute both assumptions.

## Bell-shaped Curve

IN THE early years of the twentieth century, schools operated on the notion of the bell-shaped curve. The thinking was that in any given class there would be smart students, average students, and dumb students. Within a classroom of 25 or so students, teachers were expected to grade students using a bell-shaped curve. In other words, within that classroom, there would be two or three "A" students, four or five "B" students, eight to ten "C" students, four or five "D" students and two or three "F" students. Teachers who gave a disproportionate number of "A's" or "F's" were chastised for faulty grading instead of being either complimented or assessed for the quality of their teaching. Much of this bell-curve thinking still exists in our public school system. Many teachers still expect only a few of their students to achieve "A" performance, and it is usually assumed that at least some students will not be able to achieve passing-level work. This outdated thinking is both statistically and educationally unsound.

It is statistically unsound because, as any student of statistics will point out, a group of 25 is too small to provide a normal distribution curve, so even if the idea were to make educational sense, it does not make statistical sense.

It is educationally unsound because it is exclusively based upon a supposed normal distribution of intelligence. However, in human behavior, intelligence is only one factor in a person's ability to learn and perform. Other factors, such as motivation, self-discipline, effort, and access (exposure to learning), may have as much or more influence on a child's ability to learn. "In one study of U.S. eighth graders, it was found that the best predictor of academic performance was not the children's IQ scores—but their self-discipline."[1] Moreover, if the purpose of a public school is to educate all children, then it is ridiculous to assume, at the outset, that some children will not or cannot learn.

The bell-curve structure also sets up a select-and-sort system of education. The idea is to find out who are the smartest students and who are not so smart, rather than to make sure every child is learning. Our public schools were set up, and to a large degree still are set up today, like a swimming meet rather than a swimming lesson. In a swimming meet, the purpose is to determine who is the fastest swimmer. In public schools we spend a lot of time grading students on what they have learned and then ranking them, rather than ensuring that every child has learned. What we need, however, is a public school system that is organized like a swimming lesson. In a swimming lesson, the instructor's goal is different. The goal is to make sure all students, even the slowest, learn how to swim. Swimming meets can be a result of swimming lessons, and grading can be a result of learning, but ranking students by ability should not be the primary goal of teachers or of the system as a whole.

In swimming, as in any other athletic or artistic endeavor, classes are grouped based upon the current achievement level of the students, not based on age. A swimming coach would never consider putting advanced swimmers and beginning swimmers in the same class, even if they were of the same age. Similarly, a music teacher would not put an advanced piano player in a class with beginners. It just doesn't make sense. Age is not a relevant factor in either swimming or piano lessons, but it is the overriding factor in our schools. No other major learning activity is strictly age-based. Our schools shouldn't be either.

## Curriculum

THIS SAME bell-curve thinking permeates the curriculum. To this day, textbook publishers develop textbooks designed to meet the expected average capabilities of children of a specific age. Third-grade textbooks are designed for the average eight-year-old child, as determined by a group of educators. Students in the third grade are given a curriculum based upon the average third-grade student, regardless of the learning readiness of the students in that class. The result is that some students become bored, because they are far more advanced than the presumed third-grade average, and some students become frustrated, because they are one or more years behind in their learning and are unable to keep up. In a class of 25 students, it is possible to have 20 who are below grade level and one or two who are two or three years above grade level. A teacher trying to teach a third-grade curriculum to such a class often ends up as frustrated as the students.

## Testing

TESTING IS another area in which our public education system uses group-based measurements rather than looking at individual performance. Most academic tests, whether given at the local level or applied nationally, tend to measure a student's performance compared to that of other students. "Above the national average" is a term many school districts use to evaluate their students' performance. However, being above average really does not tell the student or the parents what the student knows and is able to do. Is the national average itself at a good level, or merely a mediocre level? Who knows? Is an "A" grade given in Mrs. Wilson's class superior performance or just above average? Who knows?

Grading this way tells us which students are achieving within a particular classroom, but does not give us a clear indication of learning. Some teachers grade hard, others easy. Some high schools have high academic standards; others do not. Universities know that grade inflation has run amok in this country. They know that a 4.0 grade-point average from one high school may bear little resemblance to a 4.0 grade-point average from another. In fact, it is a well-known fact that certain high schools receive many more university acceptances than do others. Thus, where children attend high school, as opposed to their true academic achievement, can determine whether they will receive a college acceptance.

In all of these instances, the issue of learning is subordinated to the issue of ranking. Knowing who had the best test scores or who learned the fastest is not the correct measure. What we need to measure is whether every child learned. By changing our system to focus on the learning of the individual child, we will begin ensuring that every child learns. We will also ensure that every child, upon graduation from high school, will be ready for post-secondary education or for the world of work.

The problems I described are exacerbated as students grow older. By the time students are in high school, if their learning needs have not been met, in the early school years, they are likely to become so frustrated and demoralized that they drop out. Others continue, just to get by, and will graduate from high school barely able to read their own diploma. It is a crisis both for our young people and for our country, as we continue to fail to educate millions of our citizens, who are then unable to earn a decent living in our society and whose children will likely start school ill-prepared to learn. It is a vicious cycle. This under-education of our citizens is one of the main reasons we are seeing an increase in poverty. A study by the Opportunity Nation coalition found that "6 million Americans, aged 16–24, are neither in school nor working." The coalition also found that "in 49 states, the number of families living in poverty has increased, and in 45 states, household median income has fallen in the last year."[2]

The report goes on to note that "the nation's largest cities: Chicago, Houston, Dallas, Miami, Philadelphia, New York, Los Angeles, Atlanta and Riverside, California—have more than 100,000 idle youth."[3]

These young people are very likely to live their adult lives in poverty. Many will be incarcerated, and most will be dependent upon welfare, instead of becoming productive citizens who pay taxes.

The above situation is the result of our failure to effectively educate our young people. Failure to deal with the learning needs of individual children at the point where they are in their learning is a recipe for failure. We have been doing that for decades.

This group-versus-individual schooling not only fails to serve those who are behind in their learning; it fails to serve a lot of very bright children who suffer from ADHD or similar maladies. These children are often some of our smartest young people, but they are not wired to receive and process information in the same way most of us do. When a school or district has only one type of learning system, these children are also poorly served. This becomes another educational tragedy for the children, their parents, and our society.

## Tracking

ANOTHER ASPECT of group-based education is tracking. This often starts early in a child's education and is based on teacher evaluations of a student's ability to learn. Students who are behind are put on a slower track and are given a less-demanding curriculum. Once on a slow track, a student is unlikely ever to catch up. This situation causes millions of students to receive an inadequate education, one that fails to prepare them for the society in which they will live. Tracking is an outgrowth of the bell-curve thinking of the past and is still with us today.

Tracking also occurs because of a propensity for teachers to have low expectations for certain children. Children from minority communities, children raised in poverty, and children whose native language is not English, all regularly encounter teachers who expect them to perform below the level of other children. Once this occurs, it becomes a self-fulfilling prophecy.

Many minority children and many children raised in poverty are very likely to start school behind in their learning, and, if their delay is not compensated for quickly, will continue to fall behind. In fact, they will fall further behind as each year passes. However, being behind in learning is no indication of an inability to learn. All children, regardless of background or race (even those mentally handicapped), have the capacity to learn. We just need to ensure they are given the right opportunity to do so.

## Conclusion

TODAY, BECAUSE of the failure of our education system, we now have almost three generations of adults who are poorly educated or under-educated for the demands of the world in which they live. These people are often high school dropouts, often are people of color, and often live in poverty. Not only are these adults not prepared for the world of work; they are not equipped to be the kinds of parents who properly prepare their children for school. We can't blame them, but we can prevent their children from experiencing the same fate.

Suffice it to say, all children are different, and all children have different learning needs, different learning interests, and different learning readiness. A group-based learning system will never effectively educate all our children. Moving the system from focusing on groups to focusing on individual children will be a big step in ensuring the effective education of every child. One of the fastest ways to make this shift is through the increasing use of new technology in the classroom. We will discuss this issue in Chapter 10.

# 9. A Longer Day/Year and Time versus Achievement

The idea of a longer school day and a longer school year has validity only if we have corrected the other problems in the system. Instituting a longer school day and longer school year before we address teaching, leadership, and governance problems would simply provide our children with a longer, but still lousy, school year. If, however, we make the suggested changes to improve teaching quality, school leadership, and education governance, then a longer school day and a longer school year makes all kinds of sense, at least for some children.

## Longer Day and Longer Year

As stated before, America has one of the shortest academic years in the developed world. That makes no sense when we all know our children need to be educated to a much higher level today than at any time in our history. It is unreasonable to assume that our kids can learn the same amount of material in 180 days that a Korean child will learn in 190 days. We have smart children, but our short school year handicaps them.

It is even more unreasonable to assume that a child who enters kindergarten one to two years behind other children is going to catch up by going to school the same length of time as a well-prepared child. Not only do such children need much more exposure to education; it is also quite likely that going home early after school could be detrimental to their learning. Many children, who come to kindergarten one-two years behind, come from home environments where education is not stressed and where learning opportunities are minimal. Having such students stay at school longer can be doubly productive to their growth and development.

Recognizing that all our children need to learn more today than ever before, and recognizing that we have one of the shortest school years in the developed world, would suggest that we should extend the academic year for everyone. A simple change would be to extend the school day to seven hours (it is currently six hours or less) and to extend the school year to 205 days (from the current 178 or so days). If we did that, our children would spend 33 percent more time in the classroom. That adds up to four more years of schooling over a twelve-year educational period. I have no doubt our children would learn more and would be better equipped for post-secondary learning, if we simply lengthened our current school calendar (again assuming that we have qualified people in both the classroom and the principal's office).

The longer day and the longer year would also help eliminate the pressing need for remedial education for those who attend college. Currently, almost half the students who attend either a four-year or two-year post-secondary school need remediation in at least one subject. This is an enormous waste of time and resources, and it adds to an already costly effort by students to obtain an advanced education.

As mentioned earlier, the longer day and the longer year would help eliminate the current feeling that teachers are underpaid. Extending the day and year, even without changing the hourly rate of compensation, would substantially increase the yearly salary of every teacher.

Finally, the longer day and the longer year would help eliminate the achievement gap (the difference in performance between many minority children and both white and Asian children), and it would reduce, if not eliminate, the dropout problem we now face. This latter point will be explained below.

A longer school day and longer school year may not be necessary for every student. Students who are fast learners or those who come to school extraordinarily well-prepared may not even need to attend school as long as our current school year. These students should be allowed to move through the curriculum at their own pace and may well graduate at a much earlier age. This should be encouraged as opposed to discouraged, as is now the case. Regardless of a child's intellect or their learning readiness, all our children would benefit greatly from having more time to achieve the learning goals we set for them and to gain the skills and knowledge they will need to be productive adults.

## Time versus Achievement

DURING ONE of my visits to Texas, I heard a principal describe the issue very succinctly. He said:

> In the equation of education, time is the constant and achievement is the variable. What we need is to have achievement be the constant and, by definition, time becomes the variable.

*A paradigm shift! A 180-degree paradigm shift!*

Moving to an achievement-based system of learning would force a complete change in how we organize the school day and the school year, and would even change how the classroom is operated. It would also require a shift in the culture of our society. The summer break, for some students, would not take place in mid-June, but would fall later—and more briefly—in the summer.

In an achievement-based system, schools would be organized by achievement groups or levels, with class size determined by the current level of learning of the students, not by their ages. The less prepared a student, the smaller would be the class size and the more individualized the instruction. Less-prepared students would attend school for a longer day and for a longer year, until they reached a standard of learning appropriate for students of their approximate age. Only when they had learned what was required would they move on to higher levels. A good analogy to this type of educational system is the merit badge system used by the Boy Scouts. In Scouting, a young person can become an Eagle Scout at any age between 10 and 18. However, no Scout can earn Eagle rank without achieving the satisfactory completion of all the merit badges required. We thus have Eagle Scouts of varying ages, but none has failed to meet the standard.

Achievement grouping is not tracking or ability grouping, and it should not be confused with this kind of traditional grouping. Tracking and ability grouping set a student on a certain path based on the assumption that the student is either a gifted or a mediocre learner. Once on a track, the student would either be made college-ready or be given a lower level of learning designed to accommodate their abilities as assessed by others.

In an achievement-based system, it is assumed that all children can achieve at a high level. The system simply recognizes that some children have had more access to knowledge and learning than others and that some children can learn certain subjects faster than others.

## Levels, Not Grades

An ACHIEVEMENT-BASED system would not have grades one, two, three, and so on, nor would it have letter grades A, B, and C. Students would start the year by being placed in appropriate levels and would remain there until they had met the standard of learning for that level. Children behind in their learning would be put in smaller classes with gifted teachers to speed up their pace of learning. Then they would move to the next level, regardless of whether or not the month of June had happened to arrive.

For example, today a student takes Algebra I for a year, regardless of whether the child requires six weeks or 26 weeks to learn the material. The student is then graded on his or her performance relative to other students in the class. The grade is based on a standard of performance established by the teacher, the school, or the district office. A student may receive an "A" or some lesser grade, based on how the student does on the tests. The focus in our current system is on sorting and teaching, not learning. All students receive the same material, presented in the same manner, and students are graded on how well they absorb the lessons presented. The focus is also on time.

In an achievement-based system, the math student would move once he or she had mastered Algebra I, regardless of the time required. Such a system focuses on student learning, not teaching and sorting, and it has the advantage of not being constrained by time or age.

In an achievement-based system, children would be placed in levels based not on age but on their current level of learning. Achievement grouping would put students into classrooms in which all the students would be at approximately the same level of learning, regardless of age. By doing this we would allow each child to keep moving forward in his or her learning, and children would not be placed with a classroom group that was either years ahead or far behind where they were in their own learning. For example, if a kindergartner is already reading, but not doing well in math, that child may attend class at level two or three for reading, but go to class at level one for math.

Students who start school well behind in their learning would be put in smaller classes, with individualized instruction, while those at or above standard in their learning would be put in more advanced classes that might well have a larger number of students. Under this shift in approach, students who were behind in their learning would get more assistance so they could catch up, and those who were advanced in their learning would not be held back. Each type of student would be allowed to learn at his or her own pace, and would not be constrained in advancement. Also, we would use teachers' time more effectively, thereby enhancing their ability to teach and increasing their job satisfaction.

Those students who need more work would attend school longer each day and perhaps more days each year. This increased school time would be provided to help these students catch up to their peers and to minimize the variation in age ranges that could occur. Under this system, no one would be left behind, no one would fail academically, and students would not move up until they had learned what they needed to learn.

Built into this thinking is the philosophy that all children can learn, but some need more time than others. If you don't believe that, then a longer day/year would be absurd. However, if you do believe it (as I do), then it is incumbent upon us to create an environment in which every child's learning can occur in different ways and at different times and at a different pace. The assumption is also that the child is exposed to effective teaching. This latter point will minimize the time a child needs to learn material, as effective teaching has been shown to greatly enhance the pace of learning. Also, not all children would have to learn to advanced levels in various subjects, but all would be required to learn what is deemed necessary in order to be responsible citizens.

This flexible system would accommodate the five-year-old child who has been blessed with a loving and nurturing home, who has been exposed to books since infancy, who has been on a computer for three years, and who knows numbers and is reading at an elementary level by the time he or she arrives for the first day of kindergarten. It would also accommodate the five-year-old child who has never experienced a stable home environment, who has never been exposed to books, who has never seen a computer, and who may not speak English. In our present system, these two students could be assigned to the same classroom, with the same curriculum, delivered the same way for the same length of time, and we would expect them to achieve the same learning outcome. This rigid approach has never worked and it will never work. It is insane!

Creating an achievement-based system will also require a societal change. We could have 12-year-olds graduating from high school and older students getting personalized attention and attending school for a longer day and year. The former, could be mitigated by bringing college-level courses into the high school, as is now done with Advanced Placement courses and International Baccalaureate courses. If this were to be done, it could dramatically reduce the cost of college for many families.

Students who graduated early might be able to achieve one or two years of college education without ever having paid tuition. This is already occurring through another program called Running Start, which allows advanced high school students to take classes at community colleges or universities. The one disadvantage of this program is that the student has to leave high school and attend classes at the community college or university. Either idea achieves the same goal, but bringing college courses into the high school would be far more convenient, potentially less disruptive, and probably less expensive for the state. It would also keep students in buildings with students of similar age and social development.

Those students who are behind in their learning, even at the high school level, would be put in small classes with gifted teachers and might well stay in school longer each year. These students would receive extensive remediation to ensure they learned and to prevent extending their high school time beyond that of other students.

Under such a system, a standard high school diploma would no longer automatically represent a traditional four-year learning experience. Instead, high school would last as long as it took for the student to achieve standard in all academic subjects and mature in their total development. Such a system would focus on the needs of the individual student and would work to ensure that students achieved at their highest level. Moreover, students would not be permitted to fail. Students would move as fast as their ability and motivation would allow. Frustration, both for the student and for the teacher, would be minimized and student learning would be maximized. Also, if children know, at the outset, that they will remain in school until they achieve a defined academic standard, they will have great motivation to engage themselves in learning. Having to attend school while their friends enjoy the summer holiday would be a huge incentive to learn the material.

In *The Poisoned Apple*, Betty Wallace and William Graves point out that achievement grouping is a preferred educational system in three fundamental ways:

> First, it holds high standards for all students, not just some. It assumes that progress up the achievement staircase is more a function of effort than intelligence. It assumes that all students are smart enough to reach the top. No one is locked into lower levels.
>
> Achievement grouping also is fluid. It does not force students to move from one level to the next in whole groups. A student can advance whenever he is ready, whether it takes him three or thirteen months.
>
> Finally, students in achievement groups are not judged on the basis of how they compare to others of the same age. Instead, they are evaluated on what they know and are able to do and compared against a standard of performance. When they meet the standard at one level, they move to the next. There are no losers. Everyone, who tries, advances.
>
> Public schools must shift to more fluid structures and individualized instruction if they are ever to succeed in preparing all, or even most, students to be effective adults in the modern world.... The uniform, age-based U.S. public education system does not fit the nation's increasingly diverse culture.[1]

There are other elements to an achievement-level structure that make it worth attempting. First, by assessing the learning readiness of each child, it will be possible to have larger classes for some teachers, since the teacher is instructing only students who are already at or above the standard for a given level. Conversely, students who are behind in their learning would be placed in small classes where they would receive constant, individualized instruction. In both cases, money would be saved because we would be more efficient in the employment of teachers and we would have fewer dropouts, thereby improving students' future earning potential. As we know, educating our children effectively would reduce the need for many of today's social services. A well-educated citizen requires less government support and contributes more in taxes.

Obviously, schools with high percentages of children from poverty or from homes where English is not the first language would need more teachers and smaller classes. These students would also need a longer school day and a longer school year. This would obviously be more expensive and would require increased public funding to support it. However, this system would reduce the dropout rate, which would add revenues to a district. Also, other schools and districts, those with well-prepared students, could operate with larger classes and reduced payrolls. In both cases, money saved from increased efficiency could be made available to fund the students who need it the most.

The concept of eliminating both grade levels and letter grades is already occurring in several school districts. "A version of the technique has been adopted by at least 29 small districts, organizations and schools nationwide. Results show that students taught with the method are up to 55 percent more likely to pass state standardized tests."[2]

A research report in 2010, by the Colorado-based Marzano Research Laboratory, showed that "schools that use the model are 37 percent more likely to score proficient or above on state tests for reading, 54 percent more likely to score proficient or above on state tests for writing and 55 percent more likely to score proficient or above on state tests for mathematics, than schools that did not use the model."[3]

## Standards

AN ACHIEVEMENT-BASED system could work only if standards of achievement were in place. Standards of achievement for the core academic skills would need to be established for each level. With standards, and the expectation that every child will learn, the need for selecting and sorting is eliminated. A student would be at standard, below standard, or above standard. We would not need to know that Sally is smarter than David, or that Paul learns the material faster than Michelle. We would need to know only that each student has mastered the subject before being advanced to the next level.

The creation of standards is currently taking place with the adoption of the Common Core, a set of standards that has been developed by education leaders in many states. It is a voluntary set of standards that is being widely adopted throughout the country. Common Core comprises standards for English/language arts and math that could form the basis of an achievement-based system.

The Common Core standards are not without controversy. Several states have decided not to adopt them. Some people feel they are too hard; others feel they are too easy. Still others are concerned that they are just another government mandate. Regardless of what becomes of the Common Core, standards of some sort are needed to define the learning level we want all students to achieve.

In many circles, within the education community, Common Core adoption is seen as the key to improving our schools. That is a mistaken assumption. Standards will not improve schools any more than a budget will improve a business. Neither will change how the organization performs, but both help to assess effectiveness.

Unfortunately, many believe our schools will improve with more rigorous standards and that was one of the drivers for the development of the Common Core. But, poor performing schools, like poor performing businesses, need much more than standards or a budget in order to improve. We absolutely need standards to measure our effectiveness, but improving our schools is not going to occur as a result of standards. Schools will only improve if we focus on changing our obsolete system of public education. Right now, we have the "cart before the horse."

Another deficiency of the Common Core is that it a very limited start on the development of standards. The Common Core deals only with English/language arts and math. We need standards for the other core subjects like history, science, geography, etc. Also, we should not lose sight of the need to educate our children in areas that are beyond the traditional academic core. For example, all children should take a course in economics so they understand how our economy works. They should be taught financial literacy so they not only know how to balance a checkbook, but understand how to manage money and the impact of compound interest. Health and nutrition should also be taught so children know how to take care of their bodies through diet and exercise. They should take a course on civics to grasp the structure and function of government. They should take courses in the liberal arts such as philosophy and sociology, etc. Standards for these can be developed and will be needed. However, not every subject needs a standard. The creative arts, such as music, drama, etc., don't need a standard, but are still very worthwhile to learn. As discussed in Chapter 3, the "total development" of a child encompasses much more than instructing our children in the core academic subjects. It's about teaching children how to live a happy and healthy life, as a productive citizen, in the twenty-first century.

## Conclusion

TREATING ALL children the same, as we mostly do in our current education system, does not recognize how different we all are from one another. Our education system needs to cater to those differences. As Thomas Jefferson said, "Nothing is more unequal than the equal treatment of unequal people." We do that every day in every school and it must stop.

Extending the school day and the school year, and moving to an achievement-based system of education, would be a major change not only for our schools, but also for our society. It would force almost everything we know and think about our schools to change. Not only would students, parents, and educators have to change their view of school, but our entire society would have to look at education differently. Some children would have to attend school well into the summer in order to meet standards and be ready to move on. The impact on families, educators, and businesses (such as the travel and tourism industries) would be immense. It is, however, the only way for us to be serious about effectively educating every child. If that is what this nation wants and needs, then we must focus first on the needs of our children and not let ourselves get diverted by the needs and wants of adults. Also, the changes I'm recommending need not be done all at once. In fact, they should not be made

172 / Every School /

rapidly. They should occur over time, to allow both our schools and our society to adapt.

If we implement these changes, and do it right, then over the next decade we will see a change in the learning readiness of our children. At each level of learning, fewer and fewer children will be behind. As that occurs, more and more children will move with their peers and age-level differences will be mitigated. Fewer and fewer children will need specialized help, the dropout rate will diminish, and the need for the longer school day and school year will be reduced. As in Finland, children will take charge of their learning and their level of academic success will dramatically increase. At that point, the goal of effectively educating every child in every school will be achieved.

# 10. Technology

THE COMPUTER AND INTERNET HAVE GIVEN US THE INFORMATION Age—with still-unrealized potential for education. Children, at an early age, are being exposed to interconnected computers and digital tablets with which they can play games or engage in authentic learning—and they can do this at any time they desire and at almost any location. A student in central Africa can access the Library of Congress. A child in central China can speak directly and visually with a child in Minnesota. There are no barriers, no constraints on information flow and no limits on the potential acquisition of knowledge.

But schools have been among the slowest segments of our society to respond to the advantages of technology. Many years ago, someone said to me that, "It only took 45 years for the overhead projector to move from the bowling alley to the classroom." That comment may not be totally accurate, but it does reflect the slowness of schools to adopt new technologies.

The primary reason why schools are so slow to adapt to change is the lack of training provided to our teachers. If teachers are not taught to use a view graph, they are unlikely to feel a need to do so. The same is true for computers. Schools buy things that are going to be used in the classroom, so if teachers do not use computers, then districts tend not to buy them. This is not always true, as some districts have spent millions on technological acquisitions, only to find they are not being effectively implemented. Also, as Alexander Russo, a highly regarded commentator on education change, has written, "most schools are wired, but few have school-wide Wi-Fi or enough bandwidth to allow everyone to be connected at the same time."[1]

Today, most children start using computers at a very early age. Middle-and upper-class families are raising children skilled in using digital technology. Even in homes of poverty, children are often exposed to cable TV and smart phones. However, there is still very limited employment of technology in America's classrooms. The primary reason, again, rests with the ability of the teacher to effectively employ new devices and the competency of school district administrators to support them.

I don't mean to imply that technology is not being used in public education. It certainly is. We now have high-tech schools, where technology pervades every aspect of student learning. We also see computers being used in almost every school. As a system, however, technology has not revolutionized learning as it has most other endeavors. That is slowly changing, as new products and services are being developed on a daily basis for implementation into our education system.

Today there are products and services for teacher training, for curriculum and instruction, for testing and assessment, for tracking student progress, and for the financial management of schools and districts. New companies are constantly being formed to develop tools to enhance education methods. In addition, there are the social media platforms, particularly YouTube, that provide video content that may be immediately relevant to a current classroom project.

However, we have not yet seen the technology breakthrough in education that has occurred almost everywhere else in our society, but it will come. As Lillian Pace, Senior Director of national policy for Knowledge-Works, states:

> Over the next decade, our education system will experience the kind of deep disruption and reconfiguration that Amazon, iTunes and Zipcar brought to their respective industries. The concept of "school" will take many forms where learning is no longer defined by time and place. Radical personalization will become the norm as learners and families create individualized learning "playlists" and educators embrace new roles...[2]

Technology is a game-changer. It has the capacity to change fundamentally how learning takes place, how teaching is provided, and how assessments are performed.

New technology can also be very expensive, can be poorly employed, or have little or no good effect on students. For example, today we are seeing technology being implemented almost like a new fad. In 2013, Los Angeles schools decided to provide an iPad to every student. Other districts have done similar things, but not on the same scale. The Los Angeles effort was fraught with problems: "There have been questions about the exact cost of individual devices, students' demonstrated ability to circumvent the security filters on the tools—and questions about the readiness of curriculum developed by Pearson that is designed to be embedded in the devices."[3]

Obviously, the effective implementation of technology requires a lot more than just purchasing a new computer or mobile device. Wireless Internet systems have to be in place and functional throughout all buildings, support services need to be readily available, teachers need to be trained in how to use the devices, and the relevant curriculum needs to be reviewed, approved, and installed on the devices. Students need to understand their own responsibility, particularly when it comes to portable devices. If one is lost or broken, who has to pay? What if a student forgets to bring the device to class?

All of these issues showed up in the Los Angeles implementation. After spending over $500 million to purchase iPads, the *Los Angeles Times* reported, the "Board of Education held a special meeting to discuss these and other issues and ultimately slowed the rollout that began with 47 campuses."[4] On August 27, 2014, the Los Angeles School District terminated this entire program. The *Los Angeles Times* indicated that it had been a "total failure."

As in so many reform efforts of the past, new ideas become accepted as the latest "key" to improving our schools. Major effort and money are plowed into the new system only to find out that the costly change made little or no difference. Technology implementation is no exception. We know that the degree to which something is successful is dependent upon the skill and effort of those involved and the amount of planning and scheduling that is done prior to implementation.

## Training

EMPLOYING TECHNOLOGY effectively for student learning depends upon the degree to which our teachers are skilled in the use of technology and in their ability to employ it as a teaching tool. It also requires high-quality curriculum to be available online, and full support of the system. When that occurs, effective learning will occur, whether the child is in the classroom or located in some distant place.

Most new teachers have grown up with technology, so they should already be comfortable using a computer. Usually what they need is to be trained on what new technology to use and how to use it. Unfortunately, most schools of education are not staffed with professors who have great competence in technology and its employment in learning. Until that changes, our new teachers are unlikely to come into the profession ready to employ relevant technology.

The fastest way to get technology training for our new teachers would be to employ professors from a university's school of computer science to work with the school of education. That is unlikely to occur, but it would be a good idea. For now, our schools will have to hope that new teachers have learned how to use technology on their own. Teachers who have been in the profession for many years are likely to need extensive training in the use of technology.

## Massive Open Online Courses (MOOC)

PERHAPS THE largest use of technology in learning has occurred with Massive Open Online Courses or MOOCs. These are educational courses that are open to anyone and can be accessed, via the Internet, from almost anywhere. Perhaps the most well-known provider of MOOCs is Coursera, an online service started in 2012 by two Stanford

University Computer Science professors. It is now a separate organization offering over 2000 courses. After just six years of operation, Coursera has reached over 25 million students worldwide.[5]

Most MOOCs are offered by colleges, but they have started to permeate the K–12 sector as well. Employed primarily in high school courses, these online courses can allow students to study courses not available at their own school, can supplement the information provided in their current classroom, or can be treated as a core course of the school.

The most stellar example is the Khan Academy, a nonprofit formed by one individual inventor, Sal Khan. Khan develops video courses, on numerous subjects, and then makes them available to anyone in the world. Founded in 2008, the Khan Academy has grown from one employee to 150 employees. Today, there are 57 million registered users (many more use the site without registering) clicking on Khan Academy videos (many made by Sal Khan himself).[6] It is a worldwide phenomenon. Students from all over the world are tuning in to learn from one teacher, Sal Khan. Sal has had no formal training in teaching and is not certified to teach, yet has become the most effective teacher in history. Today, there are thousands of videos posted on the site. They are available in 216 countries and in more than 30,000 classrooms, and countless users link in from home or elsewhere.[7] Khan's videos have been translated into 36 languages, and now cover courses from preschool to high school.[8]

MOOCs provide the opportunity for a single gifted teacher to reach thousands of students, thereby enhancing their effectiveness and dramatically reducing the cost to the students or to the government.

Many school districts are starting to employ MOOCs. Like anything new, the roll-out is not without difficulty or problems. Determining when and how to test students is still being worked out, as are concerns about cheating. The role, if any, for parents is still being discussed. Nonetheless, MOOCs will likely see increasing deployment in K–12 schools.

Students will likely find it attractive to have flexibility about when and where they engage in coursework. They will be able to repeat lectures or lessons over and over again until they fully understand the material. Teachers will be able to reduce their time on presentation and have more time to work directly with students, thereby increasing the individualization of learning. Principals and district administrators will enjoy the increased effectiveness of teachers as well as the decrease in costs.

## Teacher Preparation

THE USE of technology in the training of teachers is as valuable as its use in the education of K–12 students. Allowing teachers to see and speak with some of our country's most effective teachers will provide would-be teachers with additional insights into their chosen vocation. Videos of gifted teachers applying their craft with real students provide an excellent training opportunity for new teachers. Being able to see different ways of teaching the same subject is also possible with technology. Live chats with the instructor in the video can now occur, thereby increasing the value of video observations.

Technology will also change the way teachers teach. They will have to change their pedagogy from teacher-centered to student-centered. Since students will have access to the same information that is available to the teacher, it will necessitate that the teacher serve as more of a coach than a "sage on a stage."

Learning how to employ technology in the classroom should now become an important component of teacher preparation. Understanding how to employ technology to enhance student learning, to assess student progress, and to determine student needs will greatly increase the effectiveness of tomorrow's teachers.

Technology will not diminish the role of the teacher, but rather reconfigure it.

## Curriculum

TECHNOLOGY IS quickly making textbooks obsolete. Publishers are putting their textbooks on discs or even making them available via the online "cloud." In either case, the student will be rid of heavy books and can access any material immediately and the publisher can update the texts on an ongoing basis. Also, with iPads or computers, students can access the material from anywhere at any time.

There is a revolution going on with regard to curriculum. Courses in all subjects are now being made available to parents and students alike via the computer. In addition, material is presented in different ways in order to meet the different learning styles of individual students. The traditional method of one teacher presenting material to a group of students for a specific length of class time and then moving on to another subject is now no longer viable. The one-size-fits-all model is going away fast. Students need not fall behind, because they can view a video or listen to a lecture as many times as needed. Computer technology truly individualizes learning. Students can sit in a chair, lie on the floor, talk, work with friends, or use any other means necessary to understand the material. They can also do it on their own time.

## Assessment

WITH NEW technology, assessing student learning is easier than in the past. Systems are now in place, that allow a teacher to assess the learning level of each student and to provide students with help on an as-needed basis. With real-time data, teachers can ensure that every child is learning. Immediate assistance can be provided at the very time the child needs help.

Testing is also easier with technology. Many online courses now come with assessment systems built into the course. In many cases, there is continuous assessment, so the student cannot move to the next portion of a course until he or she has demonstrated knowledge of prior material. This built-in assessment not only ensures that learning takes place but, negates the need to have end-of-course tests or high-stakes testing, because the student's level of learning is already known by the time he or she has completed a given course of study.

This is much different from today's testing regimen. As Tony Wagner points out in *The Global Achievement Gap*:

> Our current accountability system primarily tests how much students have memorized and can recall at a given moment in time, and there are fifty different state standards for what it means to be proficient—none of which meet the standards for work, college or citizenship in the twenty-first century."[9]

We also know that end-of-course exams are not a measure of learning, but rather a measure of memorization. This was remarkably proven when the highly selective Lawrenceville Academy conducted an experiment by retesting students after the summer break.

> Students returning in September retook their final exams from three months earlier. To be precise, faculty removed low-level material they didn't expect students to retain over the summer. On tests of just the essential concepts, the average grade fell from B+ to an F. Lawrenceville conducted this experiment for two years, with many students and several subjects. Not one student retained all of the essential concepts that the school expected every student to have mastered.[10]

My guess is that this reality is not limited to the students of Lawrenceville Academy. I believe that, if a similar experiment was conducted in a traditional comprehensive public high school, the results would be similar. Obviously, the manner by which we now assess learning is not working. Quite frankly, we are not measuring learning; we are measuring the capacity to memorize. We need a different and better student assessment system. By incorporating continuous testing as a student moves through material, it will be possible to ensure learning and eliminate the high-stakes testing that has become the norm in our schools today. Employing technology as an integral part of the educational curriculum will make that possible.

## Student Preparation

FOR MIDDLE and upper-class families, computers are integral to their way of living. Young children, in those families, are using computer devices from a very early age. These children come to school already comfortable with electronic devices and almost dependent upon them.

However, we also have a large percentage of students who may well enter kindergarten without ever having seen a computer, let alone having knowledge of how to use one. These children are far behind their peers in the use of technology and in their own readiness to learn. Again, these children will need a smaller class, more individualized attention, specific instruction on using technology and a longer school day and school year before they can be expected to catch up with their peers.

## Conclusion

TECHNOLOGY WILL revolutionize learning as it has already revolutionized most of our society. Learning has become a 24/7 activity. To adjust to this new reality, schools will have to change so they become the place where students go for further clarification of information, for in-depth study of material, for hands-on learning such as a chemistry lab or problem-solving in a math class, for music, art, vocational and technical experiences, for athletic participation and for social interaction with their peers. School will be a place where students go to learn how to think critically and communicate effectively. They will not go there to listen to lectures.

This is particularly exciting for those students who are behind in their learning, who have a poor learning environment at home, and who may well have limited access to technology. These kids will be the greatest beneficiaries of new technology in schools, because they will be able to work at their own pace, will be able to go over material again and again until they understand it, will be able to skip over material they already know, and will have access to quality instruction in every subject. Examples of this are already being seen in hundreds, if not thousands, of schools across the nation.

For example, education researcher Liv Finne describes KIPP Empower: "This elementary school in South Los Angeles uses digital technology to deliver small group instruction to groups of 14 kindergarten students and 19 first-grade students. In 2010–11, the percentage of KIPP Empower students reading at 'proficient' or 'advanced' levels increased from 36 percent to 96 percent."[11]

Other similar successes are being seen in both public and private schools across the country. These successes are proving that digital learning methods can improve the academic achievement of all students, enhance the effectiveness and attractiveness of the teaching profession, and reduce the cost of providing a good education.

We are seeing that curriculum, testing, and teaching methods are all changing. In fact, change will become the norm, just as it has become the norm in other parts of our lives. As we know, many of the jobs our children will perform in the future do not even exist today. Thus, we need students who have learned how to learn, know how to think critically and know how to communicate effectively. With great teachers and the effective use of technology, we will be able to teach all children those skills and prepare them for life in the twenty-first century.

# 11. Choice, Vouchers, and Charters

All of us have, at one time or another, been told that the solution to fixing our public schools is to provide choice in our selection of schools, to issue vouchers that would allow us to go to any school we wanted, or to make charter schools available.

All are good ideas, but I do not believe any of them, taken in isolation, are the solution.

## School Choice

When I was on the school board in Seattle, we took a serious look at our student assignment policies. These were the policies that determined where a child would attend school. The existing policies were based upon a geographical boundary around each school. If parents lived within that boundary, their child would attend that specific school. If they lived near a quality school, they were happy with the system. If they lived near a lower-quality school, they were not. This system gave the decision to the district, not the parents, regarding the school their child would attend. We decided that we needed to make a change to give our parents more say in the selection of their child's school. As we delved into the issue, it became apparent that we could not achieve an optimum solution.

In urban systems, where there are many schools within a reasonable distance of any home, the idea of choice would seem to make a lot of sense. However, one needs to recognize that many people select the neighborhood in which they live, based upon their assessment of the nearby school. Parents who make that "choice," are adamant about wanting to attend their neighborhood school—as well they should be. They exercised their choice when they selected the house to buy or apartment to rent. However, those who live in a neighborhood where their school is not up to the standard they would like are equally adamant that they should have a choice of where to send their child to school. They, too, have a valid argument. So how can one satisfy both views? Basically, one can't!

In student assignment issues, one finds that if you maximize choice, you minimize predictability. If you maximize predictability, you minimize choice. It is a dilemma that all urban school boards and district leaders face.

It is primarily an urban issue because most suburban and rural school systems do not have the concentration of people or schools to make choice a valid option. Transportation and distances make it unpalatable for most districts. However, often people move to suburbs because of the school system, so they have already enjoyed and exercised their choice.

So we come back to the urban school dilemma. As long as schools vary widely in quality, this issue will be with us. Thus, the best solution is simply to make every school a quality school, so that choice becomes much less critical. I believe we can get there but, in the meantime, it is appropriate to take a look at how to create a system of assignment that has some fairness to it.

After much debate, my school board colleagues and I determined that the best student assignment solution would be to have a choice option with a preference to the neighborhood school. Under this system, those who wanted predictability could retain it, but those who wanted other options could also have them, although to a limited extent. The limitation, of course, was the capacity of the school to accept another student.

That is the policy we developed for the parents of Seattle, and it seemed to work fairly well. Because of transportation costs, we limited choice, with transportation within a geographical area, though a much larger area than the boundaries of a single school. The boundaries we set up had at least four elementary schools, two middle schools, and two high schools within them. Within that area, parents could send their child to any school (that had room) and be provided transportation to get that child to and from the school. The net effect was to give parents choice. Those that needed transportation had limited choice, while those who didn't, had total choice. In either case, we were able to give parents some options and it did force some schools to seriously look at what they needed to do to make themselves more attractive to their parent community.

Even within that system, choice turned out to be quite limited, as the perceived high-quality schools would fill up with local children and thus provided relatively less choice to those outside the neighborhood. Regardless of the limitations, the new assignment system met our goals and provided options, though constrained, to our parent community.

As we debated the issue of choice and predictability, another reality surfaced. That reality had to do with capacity. Providing meaningful choice to parents will work only if the district has excess capacity in schools. If every school is filled to capacity, choice is greatly constrained. Most districts do not want and cannot afford excess capacity in their schools or to have extra schools, so choice is again restricted regardless of how desirable it might be. The impact of this fact is the recognition that some children, despite having choice in theory, will, in practice, be required to attend the school assigned to them by the district.

A modicum of choice also can be achieved by creating specialized schools within the public system. Schools that focus on science, music, art, international studies, etc., are quite common in many districts. Sometimes such schools are referred to as *magnet schools* and are generally open to any student in the district. These schools often are made available on a lottery basis since they are over-subscribed. Also, they are generally limited to high schools.

As you can see from the above, choice within a given district sounds like a good idea, but in practice is very difficult to achieve and, of course, one is assuming here that school boards and administrators are even open to choice.

An alternative of choice in the public schools is to give parents the right to have their children attend private schools. Religious schools are often not part of this equation because of the need to "separate church and state." (I find this a fallacious argument, but it nonetheless seems to be the rule in most states.) Nonetheless, having the choice of going to a private school sounds like a good answer to the choice question. However, in reality, it often doesn't yield much choice either. Often, private schools have waiting lists, and so new entrants have limited chance of selection. Also, private schools know that certain children cost more to educate than others, and so they can and do select students based upon the perceived cost to educate. Affluent parents are also more likely to have their child selected for admission.

## School Vouchers

MUCH HAS been written about vouchers as a solution to failing inner-city schools. The notion behind vouchers is to provide parents with a slip of paper or some other allocation that has a specific dollar value. This voucher would then be given to the school of their choice, and that school would receive, from the state or district, the value on the voucher. Basically, parents would be given the tuition money needed to send their child to a specific school. With this voucher, the argument goes, parents could select any school of their choosing and be able to finance the cost of having their child attend that school. It is another way to create choice for parents.

Again, it sounds like a great idea, but it is very hard to put into practice, for the same reasons as mentioned above. High-quality schools tend to fill up with local students or, in the case of private schools, students who come from affluent families. In either case the options for the student to attend a specific school are quite limited.

The other problem with vouchers is the higher-than-average cost to educate certain children. If every child were to receive the same voucher (in terms of dollars), then schools would naturally accept the easiest to educate students. By doing so, the school would maximize its revenue and minimize its costs.

To make vouchers work, you would again need excess capacity in the school system, and the vouchers would need to be weighted to reflect the differing cost to educate various children. Children who come to school well-prepared are quite different from children who come ill-prepared or who don't speak English or children with some type of physical or mental impairment. These latter children cost a lot more to educate. Giving everyone a standard voucher would put these children at a disadvantage in being accepted at a school.

Again, referring to my time on the Seattle School Board, we effectively put in a weighted voucher system when we installed what we called the *weighted student formula*. By weighting each student, we were able to take into account the differing costs to educate specific children. Under this system, those schools with the most ill-prepared students received the most money. With the extra money, these schools were able to fund all-day kindergarten (at the elementary level) and reduce class sizes at all levels. Both outcomes increased the attractiveness of these schools to the parents they served. Smaller classes allowed for more individualized instruction, which enhanced academic achievement.

In combination with the implementation of the weighted student formula, we also put in the choice program mentioned above. The net effect was to create a free-market system inside the public system. The budgets of schools, were now determined by both the *number* and the *type* of students who *chose* to attend. And, if students chose not to attend, the school was underfunded and had to reduce staff and cut expenses.

This new reality changed the way schools operated. Principals and staff members recognized that they needed to make their school attractive to parents or they would not be able to retain their jobs or remain at the school. This reality was vividly shown one evening when I attended an elementary school PTA meeting. At that meeting, staff from four middle schools (two of which were magnet schools), were making presentations to attract the students of the fifth-grade parents in attendance. Each school talked about its academic programs, the school culture, special programs offered, etc. It was wonderful to see. Creating competition within the public system served to improve all schools.

The schools were able to determine what types of students they wanted to attract and how much funding they needed to operate. High-revenue students (those whose students needed more time and attention to meet standards), would become increasingly attractive to schools, thereby giving their parents more choice. As schools improved their performance and as children were brought up to standard, the differences in weighting could be diminished.

Like choice, a weighted voucher could be helpful in improving schools. Both items should be part of an overall strategy of school improvement.

## Charter Schools

In recent years there has been a major push to pass charter laws in the various states. Today, some 42 states and the District of Columbia have enacted charter school laws. The city of New Orleans has the largest concentration of charter schools of any city in the country. This occurred as a result of hurricane Katrina and the devastation it created in the city's schools. In rebuilding that system, the state deregulated the schools of the city and set up an organization called the Recovery School District (RSD). Almost all the schools of New Orleans were given to the RSD, and today all 70 schools of the RSD are charters. Of those that remained with the Orleans School District, 12 are operated as charters and four remain as traditional public schools. The Orleans School District continues to own all of the buildings in both their district and those in the RSD. New Orleans is the first city in the country to have over 50 percent of the students attending charter schools.[1] In Washington, DC, 44 percent attend charter schools.[2]

Many years ago, I wrote an editorial against the passage of a charter school law in the State of Washington. My rationale for the editorial was the realization that charter schools are simply deregulated public schools. If the de-regulation of some schools is such a great idea, why does it not make more sense to deregulate all schools? I still feel that way, even though I now support charter schools in my state. I do that because it is unlikely that my state (Washington) will anytime soon de-regulate its public schools. Until it does, charter schools provide a much-needed alternative to the traditional public schools, particularly in poverty neighborhoods. They provide real choice where previously there has been none.

In most cases, charter schools are created in neighborhoods where the schools are failing or under-performing. Sometimes, a mayor or a state education department will ask a charter organization to take over one or more failing schools. By being free of the constraints of both the state regulations and the union contract terms, charter schools can operate in a way totally different from that of the public schools and, in many cases, perform substantially better.

In states with charter school laws, there are thousands of children being served by innovative schools that have a variety of strategies and curricula. Some charters are one-off schools that have been established by a group of teachers, or a nonprofit group. Over the years, charter management organizations have developed that operate multiple schools. Perhaps the best-known charter management group is KIPP (Knowledge Is Power Program). KIPP schools are now in multiple states and are producing wonderful results. KIPP schools are generally Grade 5–8 schools that serve low-income populations. These schools operate a longer day and a longer year. Students wear uniforms, teachers are carefully selected and trained, and the principals are also carefully selected and trained. In many cases, the principals are former KIPP teachers. Recently, KIPP has opened some elementary schools and is again achieving wonderful results.

In New Orleans, there are charter schools that focus on math and science, others that focus on music, and still others that focus on art. Parents have a wide array of educational options available to them, including traditional public schools. New Orleans, which used to lag behind the rest of Louisiana in standardized test scores, is now close to the top. Graduation rates from high school rose from 54.4 percent before Katrina to 77.6 percent in 2013.[3]

Innovation and creativity are much more likely to occur in a charter school than in a traditional public school, because the staff has been carefully selected and the principal and teachers are free to do what they feel will most assist their students. In this environment, teachers have higher job satisfaction, principals have more authority and parents have more choice. It is a win-win. De-regulating our public schools would lead to the same result. In essence, New Orleans has done that.

The best example of a state de-regulating its public schools has occurred in Wisconsin. There, then Governor Scott Walker and the state legislature curtailed public employee union collective bargaining rights. This made union membership voluntary, with the result that schools could now be operated without regard to the constraints of their union contracts. As a result, schools are operating with far more autonomy than they use to have, and teachers are able to teach as they deem necessary for the students in their care. Time will tell whether these changes improve student performance. My concern is that the changes were made before the state implemented the changes I have suggested in Chapters 5, 6, and 7 above, regarding teacher quality, leadership improvement, and improved governance. Without those changes, sustained improvement may still not occur.

## Conclusion

THE REALITY of our public schools is that choice, vouchers, and charters can apply only to a small percentage of our schools and of the students who attend them. State laws, transportation constraints, local demand and/or lack of access limit the impact that these ideas can have. However, if all states do what Louisiana and Wisconsin have done, then the system would be effectively deregulated and innovative schools would be allowed to develop. These can be traditional public schools or charters—it really doesn't matter. What matters is that the school has quality teachers, effective leadership, and the autonomy to provide the best education the staff can deliver. When that occurs, students learn, regardless of their socio-economic status. Supplementing that with a weighted funding system would create a major improvement in the academic performance of our nation's children.

Until we are able to deregulate our public schools, it makes sense to continue to push for choice, vouchers, and charters. Each has the potential to improve the academic opportunity for some students, and that makes them worth trying. However, we need to recognize that the solution to our education crisis lies in improving our public schools, rather than adopting ideas that merely skirt the problem.

# 12. Brain Development and Early Childhood Education

MEDICAL RESEARCHERS HAVE LABELED THE DECADE OF THE 1990S as the "Decade of the Brain." During that decade, an enormous amount of progress was made in understanding the human brain and how it develops. What was learned, along with subsequent findings, has great implications for education and for the early development of our children.

## Brain Development

THE PROCESS of educating our children is really a process of helping them develop their brain and, ultimately, their mind. Though the mind is considered by many to be more than just the physical working of the brain (it also includes such things as consciousness, intentionality, meaning, reason, purpose, judgments, decision-making, value, and will), a crucial element in shaping the human mind and the learning process, is the development of the brain.[1] All of us come out of the womb as insatiable learners. From the moment we take our first breath, we are engaged in a remarkable learning journey. Thus, understanding how the brain develops is critical to enhancing the learning of children.

In this generation, we are discovering more than ever before, about when and how the brain is developed. We are also learning how brain development depends upon both exposure to learning and nurturing relationships. In fact, nurturing relationships are crucial to brain development.

It is estimated that the human brain (the most complex three pounds on the planet) has about 100 billion neurons or brain cells at birth.[2] "The first three years of life are a period of incredible growth in all areas of a baby's development. A newborn's brain is about 25 percent of its ultimate weight. By age 3, it has grown dramatically by producing billions of cells and hundreds of millions of connections, or synapses, between the cells."[3] This is what makes the early years so vitally important. Doctors Bruce Perry and John Marceilus explain it in this way:

> During the first three-years of life, the human brain develops to 90 percent of adult size and puts in place the majority of systems and structures that will be responsible for all future emotional, behavioral, social and physiological function during the rest of life.[4]

Even in a child's initial years, some culling occurs as certain connections are used and others are not. Synaptic pruning occurs—"tuning" the brain for efficient processing. This is a time when language acquisition is important. As babies hear words, they also tune out other sounds. By age one, writes Jack P. Shonkoff, the brain will no longer differentiate between certain sounds.

> [B]y 12 months of age, the human brain can differentiate all the sounds of the spoken language(s) to which it has been exposed. As the brain goes on to develop the circuits that figure out how groups of sounds represent words that have specific meaning, it relies on those earlier circuits to distinguish one sound from another. This is often followed by the formation of circuits that make it possible to combine words into sentences and express increasingly complex thoughts over time. Thus, learning at age 2, builds on what was mastered at age 1 and, in turn, lays the continuing foundation for what will be learned at age 3 and beyond. Stated in simple terms, circuits build on circuits and skill begets skill.[5]

Nurturing relationships assume distinctive significance in healthy brain development. Children start to develop powerful cognitive capabilities, complex emotions and essential social skills in the earliest years. Nurturing environments are, therefore, essential to early learning. For example, language is learned in relationships. Exposure alone does not do it. This was learned in an experiment where young babies were exposed to tapes of people talking Mandarin Chinese. A similar group of babies were held and then spoken to in Mandarin. The latter group captured the sounds of the language without difficulty. The former did not.[6]

Learning language is, therefore, both acoustical and emotional. The human element is integral to language acquisition. Early childhood language acquisition is dependent upon both hearing the words and hearing them in a nurturing setting. Unfortunately, we have lots of children who experience neither. Jack Shonkoff, professor of human development and social policy at Brandeis University, substantiates this point by pointing out that:

> Genes determine when specific brain circuits are formed and individual experiences shape how that formation unfolds. Appropriate sensory input (e.g., through hearing and vision) and stable, responsive relationships build healthy brain architecture that provides a strong foundation for learning, behavior and health. The most important relationships begin in the family, but often also involve other adults who play important roles in the lives of young children, including providers of early care and education.[7]

Such data show up in the issues we have earlier raised about the learning readiness of children raised in poverty. These children have many disadvantages that begin certainly at birth, if not before.

For example, in a landmark study, Betty Hart and Todd R. Risley discovered that early language acquisition is substantially different in children raised in poverty and those raised in affluence. They found that the number of words heard by a baby in one household is substantially different than in another household. This difference is vividly seen when both children start kindergarten. In a home where at least one parent is a professional, a child will hear 2,153 words per waking hour. In a working-class home, the number is 1,251 words per hour. A child growing up in a welfare home averages only 616 words per hour.[8] The net effect is that over the course of one year, the welfare child will hear 3 million words and the child raised in the home of a professional will hear 11 million words. Over five years, this difference is staggering—55 million versus 15 million. The impact on IQ and school readiness is profound.

Stress is another factor that affects children raised in poverty. In those homes, often there is only one parent and never enough money to meet the family needs, so both food and housing become stress points. This stress is felt by the baby or child and can have lasting impact on development. Long-term stress damages the brain, lowers the immune response, affects sleep, makes learning and memory harder, makes peer relationships harder, and contributes to depression. "In almost every way that it can be tested, chronic stress hurts our ability to learn,"[9] reports University of Washington professor, John Medina. Obviously, long-term stress can dramatically influence the social and emotional health of a child and, therefore, diminish the learning readiness of any child entering school.

A child needs consistent, nurturing relationships in order to develop. Such relationships shape self-awareness, social competence, conscience, emotional growth, and more—all skills needed for the "total development" of the child. In fact, says Medina,

> One of the greatest predictors of performance in school turns out to be the emotional stability of the home.[10]

Today, an increasing number of our young children are being raised in environments that do not prepare them for school or life. These children are way behind before they enter the front door of school on their first day of kindergarten. They quickly dislike school and dislike learning. Prior to their senior year they are very likely to drop out. Without massive intervention early in their schooling, these children are doomed to a mediocre education and an adulthood of poverty, welfare, and even incarceration.

In earlier parts of this book, we have discussed how we need to change the K–12 system so it will work for these children. They need the longer day and year, as well as smaller class sizes. They need wonderful teachers who can convey subject matter in an interesting and engaging manner, who are nurturers, who genuinely care about these children, and who provide them with the love and the compassion that they often fail to get at home. Even if we were to fix our schools today, we would have at least a generation more of these unfortunate children. All of us need to understand the needs they have and we must ensure their needs are met. As long as we have children being raised in environments that don't prepare them for learning, we will have to have schools equipped to make up for the deprivation these children suffer in their early years.

Going forward, however, the better solution is to intervene earlier in the child's life.

## The Case for Preschool

THERE HAVE been very few federal programs that have provided the results that were intended. One partial exception is Head Start. This program, of providing preschool to under-served populations, has been shown to positively affect young children. Obviously, not every Head Start program has been successful, but where effectively implemented with caring, nurturing providers, it has been a success.

That should not be too surprising, because the data irrefutably show that high-quality early childhood education enhances a child's performance in K–12 schooling. Numerous studies have made that case. What has not emerged, however, is the uniform availability of quality preschool for those children who most need it. Though Head Start helps, it is not sufficient to reach all the children who would benefit most from early education. Even where it is effective, it is insufficient.

At both the state and the federal levels there is now increased discussion and effort being put into early childhood education. This is a very positive development, but I fear that the outcome will not be what is needed. That fear is based on the premise that the root cause of a child's lack of preparation for learning is not the child, but rather the parents. No discussion is being provided about how we, as a society, can help these parents be better caregivers to their children, thereby raising children better prepared to learn.

John Gottman is a well-known researcher who has concentrated his work on families and early childhood development. What he has learned is that intervention with parents can dramatically improve marriages and the social and emotional development of their children. Given what Gottman has learned, John Medina has suggested that, "first grade begin a week after birth."[11] In fact, the child's learning should begin with the education of the parents.

Given what we know about the importance of the home environment to the successful development of a child, it would seem prudent for our education system and our health-care system to work together to influence our future students and citizens. It should start in the maternity ward. Hospitals and obstetricians should recognize a responsibility they have of counseling new parents on what they can do to assist in the healthy brain development of their child. These new and would-be parents need to understand their responsibilities and the fact that they are not only their child's first teacher, but their child's most important teacher. A simple list of what parents can do to prepare their child for kindergarten is shown in Appendix B.

In those instances where the parent cannot or will not provide a nurturing and loving home environment, society must pick up the slack. Early childhood education and truly effective teachers can help mitigate this problem. Family, neighbors, and religious organizations can also help. Failure to do so will permanently harm the child and make the child less likely to become an adult capable of living a productive life in a civilized society. In that event the cost to society is far greater (less income earned, less money paid in taxes, unhealthy living, and possible incarceration) than would have been the cost of effective early childhood intervention.

## Early Childhood Education

GAIL JOSEPH, a University of Washington College of Education researcher, has stated:

> There are 1825 days between the day a child is born and the day she turns five and enters kindergarten. During that time, the child is learning to be a social being. Children can learn to be aggressive, or they can learn more peaceful ways to inhabit the world.[12]

How children are raised during these early years will significantly influence the type of person they will become. Thus, it is imperative that we provide all our children with an early life that will prepare them to live in a civilized society. To do that requires that we make provisions for early childhood education for those children who will not receive it at home. We should also, as mentioned above, develop programs for the parents of these children—parents who are either under-educated adults, who were failed by an ineffective school system, or recent immigrants who may not have had any formal education. In either case, their children run the risk of not being properly prepared for school and life. Today, there are millions of children and an even greater number of parents who fit that description.

Quality preschool, and early learning centers are desperately needed to fill this void. Efforts are underway in many states to provide universal preschool, but that is not what is needed. There are millions of children who are receiving excellent nurturing and learning at home. These children do not need a new state or federal program. However, there are many children who do need high-quality day care where they will receive emotional guidance, social stimulation, and language acquisition.

Politicians, and many educational activists, suggest this can only be done by establishing new federal or state early childhood program. I disagree! We have tried that with limited results and at a high cost. A better solution would be to assist existing institutions to provide this service. Organizations such as the YMCA, the Salvation Army, and similar nonprofit organizations already have extensive programs serving this need. Helping churches, synagogues, and temples set up preschools would also provide access for many parents. In addition to being less expensive than state or federal programs, programs in these institutions are more likely to be staffed by nurturing adults who can provide the children with the type of environment they desperately need. Also, more easily than in the case of federal or state programs, ineffective personnel can be removed and ineffective programs can be closed.

A possible way of encouraging the establishment or expansion of such programs would be to give a preschool voucher to parents living in poverty. The voucher would be designed to cover 80–90 percent of the preschool costs. Not funding all of the costs would ensure that parents had to put up some minimal amount of money to get their child enrolled. Having some "skin in the game," would cause parents to be more selective and more demanding regarding the type of program in which they chose to enroll their child. This would provide a self-policing mechanism to ensure programs met the needs and requirements of the parents. It would also reduce the costs.

There also is debate going on as to whether preschools need to be licensed and staffed with licensed professionals. Certainly we need some standards for these types of facilities, as a lot of parents are not sophisticated or knowledgeable enough to know what their child needs, but I would question whether we need another bureaucracy. Developing a set of standards and then setting up a small inspection staff should be sufficient.

As for the staff, given the information mentioned earlier regarding brain development, these programs need to be staffed with caring, nurturing adults rather than teachers of content. These early years are much more about social and emotional development than they are about education. What we need to ensure is that each child comes to school as a "socially and emotionally healthy child." Such a child will be able to learn quickly and succeed in almost any learning environment. Says Shonkoff:

Emotional well-being and social competence provide a strong foundation for emerging cognitive abilities. Social skills, emotional health and cognitive-linguistic capacities are all important prerequistic for success in school and later in the workplace and community. Brain architecture and the immune system also interact as they mature, which influences all domains of development and health.[13]

Parents active in their church, synagogue, or temple are the ideal types of people for providing the appropriate environment for social development. Also, providing these adults with an income as they provide a nurturing environment for the neighborhood children is a win-win situation. Nonprofits, such as the YMCA and others, are also staffed with similar types of people who help create the type of environment these children need.

In terms of our economy, this is also the right thing to do. The return on investment from early childhood education has been shown to be one of the best investments we can make. "In fact, long-term studies show that model preschool programs for children living in poverty can produce benefit-cost ratios of 17:1 and annualized internal rates of return of 18 percent over 35 years."[14]

The Perry Preschool Project (a longitudinal study that compares at-risk 3- and 4-year olds who attended preschool with those who did not) found that children in intensive high-quality preschool programs:

- Were more likely to graduate from high school.
- Were more likely to have a job.
- Had significantly higher earnings.
- Had a significantly higher rate of home and car ownership, and had a savings account.
- Were less likely to use sedatives, sleeping pills, tranquilizers, or drugs.
- Had significantly fewer arrests, and were less likely to be arrested for violent crimes or for property or drug crimes.

- Had savings in crime costs (for example, males in the program cost the public 41 percent less in crime cost per person).[15]

Early childhood education for at-risk children is not only the right thing to provide; it is an essential element to insuring the effective education of every child. As a society, we need to look at education not as a K–12 system, but as a program of child development that goes from birth until the child is capable of becoming a productive citizen.

# Part Four:
# The Need and the Plan

# 13. A Call to Action

EDUCATION IS PERHAPS THE MOST TALKED ABOUT ISSUE IN OUR SOciety. We hear about education issues from parents, teachers, politicians, union leaders, business leaders and the general public. Everyone is concerned about the education of our children, and everyone seems to have a solution or idea of what we need to do. That is not new; it has been discussed for decades. In fact, back in 1983, in the famous report *A Nation at Risk*, this comment was made:

> Our once unchallenged preeminence of commerce, industry, science, and technological innovation is being overtaken by competition throughout the world…. The educational foundations of our society are presently being eroded by a rising tide of mediocrity that threatens our very future as a Nation and a people…. We have, in effect, been committing an act of unthinking, unilateral educational disarmament.[1]

In the intervening 36 years, the discussion has continued, but the results have been negligible. All kinds of ideas and efforts have been made with no significant change in outcome.

Today, we are seeing major efforts being made to install the Common Core standards, to increase charter schools, to expand school choice, to add more rigor to our schools, to add tougher end-of-course tests and to increase funding. Some of these issues are looked upon as being solutions. Others are considered needs.

Seldom, however, is there a discussion about a fundamental change of the system and of the people who work in it. That, as I have indicated, is the real need and what should be the topic of discussion.

The increased attention to education is a direct result of recognizing how our world has changed and the implications of those changes on the learning needs of our children. Arthur Levine articulated it when he said:

America is moving from a national, analog, industrial economy to a global, digital, information economy. The two economies differ dramatically in their expectation for schools and teachers.

Industrial societies focus on common processes, epitomized by the assembly line. Our schools—products of the industrial age—rely on such processes: Schools enroll children at age 5, sort them into classes, teach them specified subjects for uniform lengths of time determined by the Carnegie Foundation for the Advancement of Teaching in 1906, and require attendance 180 days annually for 13 years.[2]

Marion Brady summarized the situation well:

America is no longer an industrial society, but our schools still operate with the "industrial" model. The focus is on teaching, not learning. As a consequence, American education isn't up to the challenge. The evidence is inescapable. Millions of kids walk away from school long before they're scheduled to graduate. Millions more stay, but disengage. Half of those entering the teaching profession soon abandon it. Administrators play musical chairs. Barbed wire surrounds many schools, and police patrol hallways. School bond levies usually fail. Superficial fads—old ideas resurrected with new names—come and go with depressing regularity. Think tanks crank out millions of words of ignored advice, and foundations spend billions to promote seemingly sound ideas that make little or no difference. About a half-trillion dollars a year are invested in education, but most adults remember little and make practical use of even less of what they once learned in thousands of hours of instruction.[3]

Brady paints a pretty bleak picture, but he is describing what many of our schools look like and what many of us experienced in our K–12 years.

Our American culture is based on some core values such as individualism, initiative, spontaneity, and creativity. We admire the independent thinker, think personal autonomy is a very good thing, and believe every person should be helped to realize his or her full potential. But we create and continue to maintain an educational system at near-total odds with what we say we believe. Instead, we standardize. Just about every school in the country—public, private, parochial, charter, magnet, virtual, home, whatever—uses the same calendar, the same curriculum, the same or very similar standards, the same nationally distributed, interchangeable textbooks, and the same corporately produced standardized tests. The lack of public protest testifies to the inability of most to realize how at odds our values are to our approach to educating.

Every student, for example, must take higher math; this despite the fact that in any randomly selected school, it's unlikely that more than a small handful will have enough mathematical ability and interest to consider making active, productive use of it. How much sense does it make to put a math whiz in an algebra classroom with 25 or 30 aspiring lawyers, dancers, automatic transmission specialists, social workers, surgeons, artists, hairdressers and language teachers? How much sense does it make to put hundreds of thousands of kids on the street because they can't pass algebra?[4]

The problem is obvious, but the solution has evaded us for decades. Many have tried and to no avail. However, the old adage "Failure is not an option" is what needs to be our clarion call to action. We've tried adjusting the present system and that has not worked. Now we must create a new system.

Changing our education system is not for the faint of heart. We need to remember that:

> We are taking on a $600 billion enterprise with more than 6 million employees. The old one-room school house has been turned into a government jobs program where the number of employees has grown four times as fast as the rate of students. Public education has become a labyrinth of political, bureaucratic and union empires that depend on a captive population of students and minimal quality control.[5]

This bureaucratic empire is very resistant to change. In my efforts, I started with the idea of changing a district and learned that it would not work at that level. Granted, you can make changes at the district level, but it is impossible to make such change last. Sustainable change is not possible at the district level because of the constant turnover of superintendents and school boards as well as the ever-present strength of unions. Leadership and governance changes are the norm in most districts, and so we must look to the state. We must look at changing the laws that now govern the present system. To do that will take political courage, something that is in short supply.

We need governors and state legislatures willing to take on the entrenched bureaucracy of both universities and unions. One state needs to step up and lead the nation in systemic change of our education system. Both Mitch Daniels of Indiana and Jeb Bush of Florida did great work on education during their respective tenures as governors. However, neither took on certification laws or governance issues, which, in my mind, is where the effort needs to start.

Today's public schools not only operate in an obsolete system; they do so with ill-qualified and ill-equipped people. We have both a systems problem and a people problem in our education system. And, like any institution, you cannot expect the people who currently operate an obsolete system to be the ones to change it. The change we need can only occur with well-trained and innovative people, most of whom will be new to the system.

We must get the right people into the teaching profession and qualified leaders leading the system before any meaningful and sustainable change is likely to occur at either the school or district level. To do that, we must start with the certification laws, increase the qualifications for those allowed to enter the profession, and develop selective and effective leadership training for both principals and superintendents. Then we must make changes in the governance model of our districts. If we take these steps, then this new cadre of talented people will begin to make the other system changes needed to make our schools perform for our children.

By eliminating certification laws and modifying the governance structure, particularly in urban systems, we can begin the process of upgrading the talent and competence of the people who enter the system. We can begin the process of selecting well-trained leaders for our schools and for our districts. We could have qualified people serving on school boards (if we continue to have them) who bring a lifetime of wisdom to the effective operation of the system. We would also make working in the system far more attractive.

Many good teachers agree that dramatic reforms are needed:

A transformed profession would give teachers much more responsibility and flexibility to make decisions that meet their students' educational needs—allowing access to and training with technology, shifting class sizes, and restructuring the school day so that they have time to collaborate with colleagues and engage in professional learning and problem solving.

We would offer teachers a professional salary and career pathways that acknowledge their skill and commitment in one of the most complex, demanding and important jobs in the world. We would insist on great school leaders, with principals who have high expectations; develop all teachers as lifelong learners; and create positive school cultures where students and teachers succeed.[6]

All this might seem like a pipe dream, but it is already happening in many schools in this country. Tony Wagner, in his excellent book *The Global Achievement Gap*, describes a wonderful charter school located outside Boston. Named the Francis Parker Charter Essential School, this school has 365 students in grades 7–12 and serves a diverse student body, with more than 20 percent of the students classified as special needs kids.

At Francis Parker they operate with a modified level program. Kids who would be in either seventh or eighth grade are in Division I. Ninth- and tenth-graders are in Division II, and the eleventh- and twelfth-graders are in Division III.

[A]ll classes are two hours in length, are interdisciplinary, and are taught by teams of two teachers in what the school calls its two Domains: Arts and Humanities; and Math, Science and Technology. All students must also take Spanish and Wellness.[7]

This particular school graduates 100 percent of its students, all of whom are accepted to college, and 85 *percent graduate from college*.[8]

Still another successful innovation is being spearheaded by the Haberman Foundation out of Houston, Texas. This foundation is working on a variety of school reforms. They have initiated a program called Fast Break. It is an innovative approach to remaking high school. Here are some of the key features of the program:

- Instructors with different specialties co-teach (2 to 4 per teaching team) and fully integrate the teaching of reading, math, communications (oral and written), computer applications, and career selection and employability skills. They also provide placement and follow-up services.

- All instructor teams stay with the same group of 25 to 60 students for most/all of the instructional day, modeling the kinds of teamwork and collaboration seen in the best companies.

- The concentrated (5 to 8 hours a day for 8 to 12 weeks) program provides sufficient time on task to produce good learning habits and prevent forgetting.

- Courseware, online testing, and small-group instruction facilitate teaching students of different ability levels at the same time.

- Highly engaging curriculum is experiential, team-oriented, and project-based, and it integrates soft skills such as teamwork, customer service, time management, and conflict resolution into the teaching of academic skills.

- There are no bells or annoying interruptions during the school day.

- Students who meet Fast Break's Achievement, Attendance, and Attitudinal requirements (the "3 A's") are rewarded with assistance in obtaining an outcome they value, such as a career-entry job, college admission, or accelerated academic credit leading to the next grade-level promotion or enrollment in advanced academic or technical training.[9]

These are examples of some of the wonderful ideas starting to be implemented in high schools. The KIPP program, mentioned earlier, has some equally impressive programs for middle-school students and is now achieving similar results at the elementary level.

In each case, what is occurring is that talented people are being given the opportunity to innovate and to create exciting and effective learning environments for students. This could happen nationwide, if we simply put the right people in the right jobs and reduced regulatory constraints. Even the constraints of union contracts can be overcome with the right kind of leadership.

If we did all of this, we could create schools like those described by the Center on Reinventing Public Education:

> In order for schools to succeed, they need to have a clear and commonly understood definition of a graduate's character and skill set. They need to be able to develop a team of people who agree on a common plan for achieving those goals. They need a fierce determination to solve problems at home or at school that might interfere with learning. They need to set and enforce norms about learning and behavior that all adults and students agree on. They need to be able to use time and money in ways that make sense for their school and their students. And they need to be responsive to parents and accountable for results.[10]

The Broad Foundation, in awarding the Broad Prize for Charter Schools to Uncommon Schools (a charter management organization), described their schools this way:

> Uncommon Schools all share key attributes: a college-preparatory mission, high standards for academics and character, a highly structured learning environment, a longer school day and a longer school year, a focus on accountability and data-driven instruction, and a faculty of committed and talented leaders and teachers.[11]

It is obvious we know what is needed. Now we must make it a reality.

We also need to remember that all children need not go to college, but they all need to be educated. Today, welders and plumbers need to know geometry and some chemistry. Kids not planning on college need to have other career opportunities exposed to them, while still in high school. In my day, we had wood shop and metal shop as well as mechanical drawing. Today, we probably need an electrical shop, plumbing shop, computer-aided design shop, computer hardware shop, etc.

Back in the early 1990s, I participated in the creation of the Thomas Jefferson School for Science and Technology, which was designed as an applications-only public high school in Fairfax County, Virginia. This high school, which was enormously successful from the very beginning, is still a sought-after school today. At TJS, we created several labs for the students to have hands-on engagement in specific work areas of interest. The labs included a biotechnology lab, a telecommunications lab, an applied materials lab, a computer science lab, and several others. Today, that same school has twelve such labs available to the students. Though the students in this high school were all being prepared for college, the labs were wonderful learning areas for any student interested in those particular disciplines. Similar labs could become part of high schools as we move further into the twenty-first century. Such labs could be easily staffed with talented people if we eliminated certification laws and allowed experts from specific trades specialties (electrical, welding, programming, etc.) to work in our schools.

Preparing our children for the world of either work or advanced education is a primary responsibility of the present generation of adults. As you have read, we are not meeting that responsibility. This is not the children's fault, as our children are every bit as capable as any children in the world. We just need to give them the educational opportunity to excel. Educating our children should be our highest priority, and we should have our brightest people engaged in that endeavor. We should also make sure those bright people have the freedom to innovate and the incentive to perform. They need to be well-led and well-governed. All we need now is a plan to make it happen.

# 14. The Game Plan

AS MENTIONED EARLIER, OUR PUBLIC SCHOOL SYSTEM IS A HUGE ENterprise. Changing such an enterprise cannot be done by fiat; it cannot be done uniformly; it cannot be done as one major effort and it cannot be done quickly. Huge systems take time to change and this one will be no exception. We should expect and plan that it will take time, likely years, to see a total system change, even in one state. However, we need to approach the effort with a sense of urgency and move at the maximum pace appropriate for complex systems. As we approach this task, we need to keep several points in mind.

To begin with, we have learned that children learn in different ways and at different times in their development. This reality tells us that a new system must be different than the "one size fits all" system we have now. We will need many different approaches to improving our schools. Allowing innovation to flourish will be essential to success. Yet we must expect resistance to such innovation, coming from several quarters.

First, we must recognize that our education system is also a major component of our American culture. We Americans are used to our children going to school six hours a day, being off for a couple of weeks over Christmas, having a winter and spring break and the summers off. This calendar has not only influenced how families live and travel, but has created a huge travel and tourism industry that would fight very hard if we tried to quickly make any major change to the school calendar.

Second, a major constraint on reforming our school system is the unions. Though I have said, in Chapter 4, that they are not the source of the problems in our education system, they are most certainly the biggest constraint upon fixing them. Unions tend to abhor change and fight to preserve the status quo. That is unlikely to change. In those states where unions are strong, change is likely to be the most difficult to achieve.

Third, we also need to recognize that not all children are being failed by the present system. In fact, this country regularly produces some of the smartest people in the world. Middle and upper-class parents know how the system works, and they make sure their child receives a good education. This is done by using "choice": deciding where to live (picking a neighborhood with a good school system); finding out who the best teachers are and making sure their child gets in those classrooms; providing extra tutoring, if needed; and in some cases, selecting a private school. About 30 percent of our nation's children fit into this description. Parents of these children don't need schools to change. In fact, they will fight to make sure they don't change, as their children are being well-served by the present system. Therefore, resistance to change by the affluent and successful members of our society is another obstacle in any effort to transform the system. These people vote in every election and they will not be favorably disposed to candidates who threaten to change their schools.

Given the three sources of resistance indicated above, to which must be added the normal bureaucratic resistance to institutional change, it is obvious that we are embarking upon a daunting challenge.

Nonetheless, when 70 out of every 100 children are being failed by our present education system, it cries out for change to occur. About 20–25 of those 70 children will drop out of high school and the remaining 45–50 will graduate without the skills necessary to either go onto higher education or enter the world of work or enter the military. It is these children (70% of all our children) that our system is failing and it is these children who need a different educational experience.

So, where do we start to fix the problem? Originally, I thought the entity of change was the urban district. Serving eight years on the Seattle School Board (1993–2001) allowed me to test that assumption. As recounted earlier, during that time, my colleagues and I, along with an extraordinary Superintendent, were able to dramatically change the Seattle Public Schools. However, in the years since 2001, new school board members and new superintendents have virtually reversed all the changes we made. Basically, I served eight years for naught. I'm not alone in that regard. Hundreds, if not thousands, of school board members have had the same experience. In fact, it is hard to find a district, of any size, that has been able to execute a long-term plan of school improvement. Policies passed and leadership hired by one school board can easily be changed by the next. Thus, locally established rules and regulations are not sustainable.

If we want sustainable change, it must occur at the state level, with passage of new laws and codes. Because of the size and complexity of our education system, these changes have to be made in stages, so as to minimize the objections of the 30 percent who like the present system, to prevent unions from mobilizing resistance and to minimize the disruption to those industries that have benefitted from our present school calendar. What is needed is to develop a *movement* for change as opposed to a top-down dictum. The plan outlined below could take 10 years or longer to implement, but the important thing is to have a plan and to begin to execute that plan to ultimately achieve the desired outcome: *a school system that effectively educates every child.*

The plan outlined below challenges the *status quo* and maximizes the impact of every dollar spent. The reforms are primarily policy changes. *They do not require additional government funding.* They do, however, require courageous policy-makers—primarily at the state level—who will take our recommendations to heart and put them into action. Beginning in broad-brush strokes, our policy prescriptions aim to:

- Change an adult-focused system to a student-focused system;
- Change an input-focused system to an output-focused system;
- Change a teaching-focused system to a learning-focused system;
- Change a group-focused system to an individual-focused system; and
- Change a time-focused system to a competency-focused system.

# Phase I (1–3 Years):

So how do we propose to change an entrenched system with well-funded defenders? By beginning with achievable, short-term objectives in states that are ripe for reform. We believe that these incremental steps can be realized in target states within the next few years.

## 1. Right-to-Work Legislation

In states where unions exercise sole authority over employment, compensation and working conditions, they are in a position to stop any reform efforts. Thus, if we want to begin now to improve our schools, it will likely have to be done in those states that are already Right-To-Work states. Even there, unions have often retained control over the work force (due in large part to mediocre management), so change is hindered. The Supreme Court's ruling, on the Janus case, does not change this reality, but it does help. We now have 28 states with "Right-to-Work" laws in place. Those are the states where the school transformation movement can start now.[1]

## 2. Choice Legislation

The next step is to adopt "choice," as it seems to be the easiest change to implement. It is hard to defend the notion that parents should not have a say in where their child attends school. Virtually every other aspect of raising a child is based upon the decision of the parent. What a child eats, where she lives, when she sleeps, who her doctor is, what books she reads, etc., are all decisions made by parents. However, the formal education of the child, which is probably the most important aspect of raising a child, is not currently a parental choice. We need to put the parents or guardians in charge of their child's education. Choice is the first and easiest step to allow that to occur.

Currently, there are several exciting programs being installed to provide choice to parents. One of the best is to provide "Education Savings Accounts" (ESAs) to citizens within a state. ESAs are similar to vouchers in that the state provides a fixed amount of money to the parents of each child. This money can then be used, by the parents, for payment to a school for the education of their child. In most cases, ESA money can be used for public schools, private schools, religious schools, and even for home schooling. Parents control where their child goes to school and which school is paid for their child's education. ESAs are a growing program in several states. ESAs enhance choice and they also improve the manner by which schools are funded. Both enhance a student's chance at an improved education.

Charter schools are another example of using choice by giving parents options other than the traditional public school. As indicated earlier, charter schools are simply deregulated public schools. Until we can deregulate all schools, charter schools offer parents some innovative options.

One of the constraints on full choice being available to parents is the need for excess capacity. To exercise choice, a parent must have options. These could be other schools in the same district, charter schools, private schools, etc. In each case, however, there has to be room for the child. Most districts cannot afford excess capacity, so choice is limited. Also, private schools and charter schools often have waitlists, which further limits choice. Even though these issues exist, it is still no reason to withhold choice. Parents deserve the right to control where their child goes to school, if they can.

Legislatures should pass laws allowing for school choice and the use of ESAs makes that type of legislation even more meaningful. For more on the subject of choice, see Chapter 11.

### 3. Innovation Schools and Districts Legislation

As discussed earlier, we have a school system that was set up over 100 years ago. We also have a system that is failing about 70 percent of our children. Obviously, we need to improve the performance of our schools. The question is, "how should schools be configured and operated?" There is no one answer to that question, nor should there be. What we need is to allow for the creation of new models, some of which will undoubtedly work better than others. Unleashing the best minds we have to create schools that dramatically enhance academic achievement should be allowed and promoted. Today, that is not possible, with the exception of charter schools. I support charter schools, but I also support the notion of allowing innovation to occur in the existing public system, both at the school level and at the district level.

To do this will require legislation that allows schools and/or districts to propose innovative alternatives to traditional methods. Such proposals, if approved, should grant waivers to the school or district so that current laws, codes and union contract terms can be waived. Both Mississippi and Kentucky have passed this type of legislation. Six states have also passed legislation allowing for the creation of "Innovation Zones." In Colorado, which passed a state law in 2008, Denver Public Schools had 38 "innovation schools" by 2016.[2] Memphis and Indianapolis have also allowed innovation. In each case, a few districts and/or schools have been granted permission to create different school models.

Examples of innovation could include:

- Waivers for the length of the school day and the school year.
- Waivers allowing for a change in graduation requirements moving to competency measures rather than credits.
- Waivers from any mandated salary schedules to allow different compensation systems that reward excellence and remove mediocrity.
- Waivers that allow for the hiring of non-certified teachers and principals.
- Waivers that allow a school or district to use a different curriculum than that mandated by the state.
- Waivers from standardized tests so that other measures of competency can be employed.

One district, approved for "Innovation District" status, is Corinth, Mississippi. This district has made major changes, all designed to enhance the learning of students. Corinth now operates on a revised calendar that involves four 9-week blocks, with three 3-week sessions where students who are behind, or students desiring additional learning, can remain in school, thereby extending the year to 210 days. The Christmas break remains and the summer vacation is still available, only it is shortened. Because of the waivers, Corinth has also changed its curriculum and is using the Cambridge Education System, which is more rigorous than the state-approved curriculum. Graduation requirements have been changed and Corinth now offers seven different diplomas. They are now in the planning stage for a new compensation system for teachers. It is too early to assess the impact of these changes, but every change has been well thought out and was implemented for the sole reason of enhancing the learning of the students. The teaching corps has been involved in every aspect of the transformation, so all the changes have the full support of the staff.

Innovative schools and districts require change-agent leaders as well as staffs that desire to do things differently. In the case of districts of innovation, you must also have a school board willing to take risks and a very supportive community. Both take time to develop.

However, when schools and/or districts decide to innovate, they tend to build schools that parents want for their children. When this occurs, demand increases and the movement begins.

Passing legislation to allow for the creation of innovation schools and districts is the best way to start the process of school improvement. We have seen this in the charter school movement, and it can more rapidly occur within the existing public school sector, if given permission. At least six states are leading the way.

## 4. Leadership Institute Legislation

Passing legislation to allow for "innovation districts" is only going to be of value if there are effective school leaders who are willing to innovate. Unfortunately, public education has a very limited supply of such leaders. The reason is that the system does not work to create them. In fact, the system almost works to do the opposite. School leaders, whether they are principals or superintendents, are not trained to lead their school/district. They are trained to manage their school/district. The difference is that a leader will look for ways to improve performance, will innovate, and will not be satisfied with the *status quo*. Managers, on the other hand, are trained to take what they have and make sure it continues to perform (and, hopefully, improve). We have lots of managers in education, but very few leaders.

What is needed is a new type of leader: a "change agent." In a way, we are looking to create educational entrepreneurs who think of doing school differently, leaders who will not be satisfied to effectively educate only a portion of their students. These leaders have to possess a vision of what their school or district could look like and have an understanding of what will be required to achieve that vision.

Organizational change requires superb leadership. It requires leaders with vision and great communication skills. It requires leaders who know how to build coalitions, who engage all levels of an organization in the change effort. Principals and superintendents in innovation schools and districts will be CEOs of their organizations. They will have to understand finance and budgeting (something not taught today), as they will control their school's or district's funds and the allocation of those funds. In addition, they will be responsible for the hiring and evaluation of staff and building an effective organization.

These new education leaders will also need to know how to mobilize communities, not just their own organization. These are rare talents and they are not readily available within the existing workforce of our schools and districts.

Developing that type of leader is not possible with the system we have today. That's why I earlier stated that we get "leadership by accident, not by design" in our public education system. We need a new approach to both the selection and training of education leaders.

My suggestion is to create "Institutes for Educational Leadership." These institutes would have extraordinarily high admission standards and would be populated with instructors from business, education, and public policy schools as well as leaders from business, the military, and current school systems. Significant on-the-job training would be part of the curriculum. Principal candidates would come from our most gifted teachers, who have shown not only outstanding teaching ability, but also leadership skills. Similarly, principals who had already shown an ability to develop an outstanding school, within the current system, would be selected to become superintendents. Others, with similar leadership success, in business, government, military, or central offices, would also be considered for admission.

To incentivize these teachers and principals to go back to school, they should remain on the payroll of the state and should not pay tuition while they are being developed into the leaders we need. If desired, these candidates could be treated like applicants to the military academies who sign on for a four-year, post-graduation commitment, prior to attending school. Their training should include both classroom and school/district-based training. Such a program need not be a degree-granting program, but it could be. The important thing is that it be effective in both selecting and training the leaders we need to create and operate the schools we need.

Given the nature of these "institutes," it would probably be best that they be associated with, but not part of, a major university. I say that because universities are every bit as bureaucratic and resistant to change as public schools. These new institutes need to be flexible and innovative. They also need to be formed quickly, so that the leadership selection and training can begin. They also need to be able to hire and fire as needed.

The goal would be to create leaders "by design" who will then create whole new types of schools for the 21st century. These leaders would be placed in schools or districts that need and want change or in schools/ districts that have already received permission to become an "innovation district/school" or desire to be granted "innovation district/school" status.

## Phase 2 (4–10 years):

IF PHASE 1 has been accomplished, then there are many other options that are available, all of which will serve to enhance our schools and the teaching profession. However, Phase 1 needs some time to work. What we are trying to do in Phase 1 is to start a movement. To do that, will require some time for the innovative districts/schools and our new leaders to show results. Once that starts to occur, parents will start asking for more schools that operate in a similar fashion and the movement begins.

Because change is difficult and takes time, stability of leadership is critical to the process. Currently, stability is very difficult to achieve, particularly in urban centers. As pointed out in Chapter 7, the current governance structure almost invites turnover, which in turn prevents multi-year reform efforts. Thus, the only place you will find change occurring is where there is stability of governance and stability of leadership. One begets the other.

### 1. Appointed School Board Legislation

Elected school boards, particularly in urban systems, tend to prevent long-term planning because every few years, new members are elected with a new agenda. The net effect is the preservation of the *status quo*. Today, you are hard-pressed to find an urban district that has been able to implement a long-term plan of school improvement. There are exceptions, such as Denver, Long Beach, and Montgomery County, but these are the exceptions, not the rule. The regular turnover of school board members results in constantly changing visions. This in turn produces constant revisions of plans and sometimes changes in leadership. The end result is the retention of the *status quo*. It happens everywhere.

This legislation, initially, should apply only to urban districts. It is those districts that have the greatest need for leadership and governance stability. Urban districts tend to have demographic factors historically tied to low student achievement, including poverty and a majority of students from minority populations. They also employ thousands of people and have budgets ranging from hundreds of millions to several billion dollars. These districts are very difficult to manage and tend to have high leadership turnover, resulting in the lack of a consistent plan. As indicated earlier, the average tenure of an urban superintendent is 3.1 years. By going to appointed boards, we can put in board members who will coalesce around a common agenda, who will appoint effective superintendents (from our Leadership Institute), and who will retain those leaders for extended periods of time. Stability of leadership and governance are critical to sustainable school reform.

My suggestion is that the mayor appoint the members of the board, but that the city council or equivalent body approve the appointments. This would reduce the chance that special interests will influence the selection process. This has been the process for most of the cities that now have appointed school boards (NYC, Boston, Cleveland, Chicago, Baltimore, and Washington, DC). However, in some cities, you have mayors who do not have the confidence of the state legislature. Also, you can find a city or cities where the city council is dysfunctional. In those instances, the legislature may want to retain control over the appointment of the school board. One could envision legislation that called for the governor to appoint three members, including the chair, and that each house of the legislature appoints one member each. If the board has seven or more members, as some school boards do, the legislation could be modified to accommodate that.

An even more radical idea would be to eliminate school boards entirely and let the superintendent serve on the mayor's cabinet like the police chief and fire chief. Schools are the most important institutions in any city, but they seldom report to the mayor. If that changed, mayors and city councils would take a far greater interest in having excellent schools. Proponents of "local control" might find this idea abhorrent, but local control (in major cities) is a thing of the past. Elected school board members, in large cities, often represent multiple neighborhoods, some of which they may never visit.

Regardless of the process, the end result must be to achieve stability of leadership and governance. That is not happening now, and it must happen if we expect to transform our schools.

## 2. Certification Laws Legislation

In Chapters 5 and 6, we pointed out the impact that certification laws are having on the quality of both our teachers and our school leaders. These laws give education schools a monopoly position over the supply of human capital (both teachers and administrators) allowed to work in our schools. Initially, the laws might have had merit, but they no longer achieve their intended purpose. In fact, they are doing more harm than good. They not only do not guarantee a quality teacher in every classroom or quality principal in every school; they are tending to discourage our best and brightest from even entering the education profession.

As indicated earlier, the selection and preparation of teachers and education leaders is simply inadequate. Teaching is the easiest profession to enter, whereas entrance to the profession ought to be highly selective. Quality teaching requires quality people who are well trained. With some exceptions, we are not getting enough such people.

The current certification laws no longer work and so should be modified or abolished. Education colleges need to be able to exist on their own merits, not on the basis of mandatory attendance. Removing or modifying certification requirements will open up the profession of teaching to those most qualified to teach and will do more to enhance academic achievement than anything else we can do.

This legislation will not be easy to pass, as the public believes that "certified" is synonymous with "qualified." Thus, they will support the retention of a "certified" teacher in every classroom. This attitude will not be easy to change, but could be changed by the increase in performance of the innovation schools and districts, all of whom will be hiring teachers based upon their qualifications, not their certification. As these innovation centers achieve results, not seen elsewhere, parents and voters will come to see that "certification" is not a requirement for success.

Initial legislation should simply allow schools to hire non-certified teachers. This would be the least threatening manner to begin this process. Ultimately, a legislature could simply pass legislation eliminating the notion of "certified" or pass legislation that would allow a non-certified teacher to teach and then become "certified" through proven success in the classroom. Either action would allow our best and brightest to become teachers.

Resistance to this type of change will also come from education colleges, who will have to compete for students as opposed to having a monopoly supply chain. Most of the 1400+ colleges of education would not survive a change in certification requirements. With modification or elimination of these laws, education schools would either dramatically improve or close. Either outcome would be beneficial to our students and the teaching profession. Those that did survive would be centers of excellence in the training of teachers. They would also have much higher standards of admission. Colleges of education should have to justify their existence based upon their proven ability to enhance a person's teaching proficiency. Today, that is not the case and, as a consequence, we have hundreds of education schools that fail to produce high quality teachers.

Modifying certification laws will not only enhance the quality of persons who enter the profession of teaching, but will also increase the stature of the profession. As more and more qualified people become teachers, it will raise the image of teachers, and will attract ever-better candidates.

### 3. School Funding Legislation

In most states, the funding of schools is done through the transfer of state money to districts. The funding is based upon the number of students in a district, and then the district allocates the funds to schools based upon staffing of those schools. In most cases, the principal of a school has little or no discretionary funding. Quite frankly, this system of money allocation is necessary, as most principals have no training on how to manage a budget or how to hire staff.

In addition, much of the money received by a district, from the state, comes with restrictions on how the money is to be spent. This is the result of decades of mistrust, at the legislative level, because of the mismanagement of money by superintendents and school boards. So, even at the district level, there is limited flexibility in the spending of funds. This funding system greatly constrains innovation. One can't blame states for allocating money this way, as legislators have learned that districts cannot be trusted to spend money as the legislature desires, unless there is a law or code that mandates it. Thus, they create laws and codes that specify how state money is to be spent. However, this response does not fix the real problem, which is the competency of the leadership receiving the funds. Effective leadership, at both the superintendent level and the school board level, would mitigate this need and allow money to flow to where it is most needed. The proposed Leadership Institute and the proposed legislation on appointed school boards are designed to address this issue.

To change the current funding model, a state needs to pass legislation that changes the way money flows to schools. This assumes that the state has also changed the way leaders are selected and trained. My recommendation is a system that has the money follow the child, and also takes into account both the cost of living where the child lives and the cost to educate the child. Earlier, we discussed the "weighted student formula" system that we installed in Seattle in the mid 1990s. This system took into account the differences in the cost to educate various children.

A similar system, perhaps a "weighted" ESA system, could be installed at the state level and give both districts and the individual school great flexibility in how they spend their money. Assuming that "choice" legislation has been passed, the funding of a school would then be a function of both the number and type of children who showed up.

Under this system, schools with the most difficult-to-educate population of children would receive the most funding. Also, schools would quickly realize they had to create a school that parents wanted their children to attend; otherwise, they would not get funded. Basically, this system creates a "free market economy" inside the public system.

Funding schools this way also gives school leaders the flexibility to extend the school day and/or school year. This would be particularly helpful for those students who are behind in their learning. These students need more time to meet standards, and that should be allowed. Treating these students the same way we treat well-prepared students not only does not work; it does not make sense. Yet that's what is normally done. Districts/schools that focus on student learning need the flexibility to extend or modify the time some children spend in school.

## 4. Teacher Compensation Legislation

Virtually all states have a salary schedule for their teaching corps. This schedule is usually based upon the teacher's length of service and the number of degrees the teacher has earned. None of these schedules reward excellence, and there are no promotion ladders that would allow a teacher to earn more based upon excellence in the classroom. This type of compensation system tends to reward mediocrity and discourage excellence. We need a compensation system that does just the reverse.

Innovation districts and schools will have the opportunity to hire the teachers they want, and they will have the right to pay them what they need to pay them to get them to join their school/district. This is how private schools operate, and most charter schools as well. Thus, teachers are hired and retained based upon their ability to contribute to the school's mission, not based upon length of service or some union contract requirement. In most cases, these schools hire teachers on contracts of one-year duration and the teachers are evaluated based upon their ability to teach and to have children learn under their care.

As these types of schools expand in numbers, it will become obvious that the state salary schedule is no longer needed. Hiring and compensation will be based upon the market conditions and some teachers will, therefore, make more than other teachers. This happens in every other work place environment and it should happen in education as well.

Without a mandatory state salary schedule, the local district or school becomes the hiring entity. Each school becomes like a small business in that it hires and pays its employees based upon need, market conditions and budget allowances. High-need teachers, like math and science teachers, will be paid more.

Benefits, such as medical, pension, etc., are probably best managed at district level, but could be managed at the school level if desired. The more decisions managed at the local level, the more differentiation you will create between schools.

Inherent in this reform is the right to terminate non-performing teachers. Schools should not be required to retain teachers who do not perform or who simply do not fit the culture or goals of a particular school. Effective leaders will minimize this eventuality by knowing how to hire the right people in the first place.

### 5. *Graduation Requirements Legislation*

Since 1904, we have had a common graduation requirement based upon achieving a fixed number of "credits." To earn a credit, a student must achieve a passing grade in a subject in which she has spent 9900 minutes of seat time. The student not only has to earn a certain number of credits, but also has to earn them in certain subjects (four credits in English, four credits in math, three credits in history, three credits in science, and so on). Up to 24 credits are required for graduation. All students must achieve the required credits to graduate.

This measurement system served us well during the first half of the 20th century. It is not serving us well now. Today, too many students are graduating from high school without the knowledge needed to become a productive citizen in our twenty-first-century economy. Though this has been the case for years, there has been very little effort put forward to alter the current set of required credits. What should a high school graduate *today* know and be able to do? Should we only have one kind of diploma? These and many other questions remain unanswered in most states.

What is needed is for a state to take on the task of defining what it should mean to be a high school graduate. My suggestion is that three task forces be set up, to determine the admission requirements for a university, a community college, and the workforce. In each case, the requirements will differ, as they should. This, in turn, means we should have at least three different diplomas that provide the receiving organizations with a clear knowledge of the student's capabilities. Defining what would be required to earn each diploma is the task of the state. How schools get the students to achieve those standards should be left to the school/district to determine.

Getting rid of the current credit system is the first step in changing graduation requirements. States should decide, as mentioned above, what standards need to be met and what diplomas will be given. With this change, high school graduation will mean something and will allow employers and colleges to assess the preparation each student has received.

## Conclusion

As STATED earlier, transforming our schools is going to take a while. It will require a lot of effort by many people, but it can and must be done. The process needs to start at the state level and with the state legislature. The legislative acts mentioned above are my suggestions on how it should be done and the order in which it should occur. This "game plan" is a multi-year strategy that will require strong leadership in both the legislature and the governor's mansion. Only a few states are now positioned to begin this process, but we only need one. If one state begins this transformation, it won't take too many years for it to be replicated.

The measure of any society is the degree to which it loves, nurtures, and educates its children. Today, we are failing at all three. It cannot continue and it need not continue.

We need to educate all of our children so they can grow up to be productive citizens in the twenty-first century and so they can become loving and nurturing parents to their own children. There is no greater need facing our nation. Let's begin now to transform our education system. Our children and our country are counting on us.

# A. Seattle's Union Contract Table of Contents

## TABLE OF CONTENTS, 2015-2018 SPS/SEA COLLECTIVE BARGAINING AGREEMENT

SECTION I: No Reprisal for Disclosing Misdeeds

## ARTICLE IV: PROVISIONS FOR COMPENSATION AND WORK HOURS

SECTION A: Basic Employment Contracts & Employee Responsibilities
SECTION B: Types of Employee Contracts
SECTION C: Basis for TRI and Basic Salary
SECTION D: Time Responsibility and Incentive
SECTION E: Supplemental Contracts for Stipended Assignments
SECTION F: Salary Schedule Placement
SECTION G: Miscellaneous Salary Provisions
SECTION H: Traffic Education

## ARTICLE V: SUBSTITUTES

## ARTICLE VI: LEAVE RULES, REGULATIONS AND PROCEDURES

SECTION A: Short Term Leaves
SECTION B: Long Term Uncompensated Leaves
SECTION C: Leave for SEA Officers

## ARTICLE VII: EMPLOYEE BENEFITS & PROTECTION

SECTION A: Group Insurance Provisions
SECTION B: Liability Coverage and Hold Harmless Provisions
SECTION C: Protection of Employees, Students and Property
SECTION D: Travel Allowances
SECTION E: Transportation of Students
SECTION F: Tax Sheltered Annuities
SECTION G: Transit Passes

## ARTICLE VIII: STAFFING–QUALIFICATIONS-BASED HIRING FOR CERTIFICATED NON-SUPERVISORY EMPLOYEES

SECTION A: Staffing Decisions
SECTION B: Three-Phase Staffing Process
SECTION C: Site-Based Hiring Process
SECTION D: Hiring Process for Certificated Non-Supervisory Personnel Other Than Teachers
SECTION E: Mid-year Transfers
SECTION F: Administrative Transfer Procedures
SECTION G: Special Staffing Issues at Schools Requiring SPS Intervention
SECTION H: Program Movement or Closure
SECTION I: Employees Covered Under Section 504 of the Rehabilitation Act of 1973
SECTION J: Affirmative Action

## ARTICLE IX: WORKDAY, WORKLOAD, ASSIGNMENT AND SCHEDULING OF EMPLOYEES

SECTION A: Length of Workday

## ARTICLE X: GRIEVANCE PROCEDURE

## ARTICLE XI: EVALUATION

## ARTICLE XII: LAYOFF AND RECALL

SECTION B:    Seniority
SECTION C:    Displacement and Layoff Guidelines
SECTION D:    Certificated Employee Layoffs
SECTION E:    Recall from Layoff: Provisions for Reemployment of Laid off
    Employees
SECTION F:    Employment Notification
SECTION G:    Recall from Layoff and Seniority

## ARTICLE XIII: NO – STRIKE CLAUSE

## APPENDICES

A:    Certificated Non-Supervisory Employees Salary Schedule 2015-2016
B:    Time Responsibility and Incentive
C:    TRI Contract
D:    Extra-Time Hourly Rates 2015-2018
E:    Special & Supplemental Assignments Compensation Schedule 2015- 2018
F:    School Year Calendar 2015-2016
G:    Teachers' Responsibilities
H:    Danielson's Framework for Teaching Rubrics
I:    Washington State Criteria Student Growth Rubrics
J:    Certificated Teacher Classroom Observation Form
K:    Comprehensive Evaluation – Danielson – Certificated Classroom Teacher
L-1:    Professional Growth Support Document
L-2:    Performance Improvement Plan
M-1:    Professional Growth Support Document – ESA
M-2:    Performance Improvement Plan – ESA
N:    Certificated Teacher Summative Evaluation Form
O:    Performance Schedule for Teachers on Provisional Contracts
P:    Goal Setting Form
Q:    Guidelines for Evaluation of Substitute Teachers
R:    Substitute Evaluation Form
S:    Best Practice for Substitute Teachers
T:    SEA/SSD Contract Waiver Request Form
U:    MOU Regarding Focused Evaluation Scoring for Non-Supervisory
    Certificated Instructional Staff
V:    MOU Regarding Final Summative Evaluation Performance Ratings for
    Non-Classroom Certificated Employees
W:    MOU: Amnesty Agreement
X:    Letter of Agreement: Recess
Y:    MOU: 20 Minutes of Instructional Time
Z:    Special Education Relief Fund Request Form
AA:    Substitute Incident Report Form

# B. Preparing Your Child for Kindergarten

1.  **Read to and with your child every day.** Reading to and with your child helps your child learn and understand language. Active reading is best. Discuss what you read or see in the book.

2.  **Talk with your child throughout the day.** Conversation not only engages your child, it builds vocabulary and will help your child talk and learn.

3.  **Establish routines and follow them consistently.** Children need structure. It provides safety and reduces stress so that your child's young brain can absorb information.

4.  **Be positive when giving instructions. Focus on the "Do" and not on the "Don't."** Learning should be fun, not painful.

5.  **Establish behavior expectations starting at age two. Before starting something new or different, tell your child what you hope for and then be consistent about the expectations.** Children face expectations all their lives, beginning with preschool or kindergarten. Expectations should be explained in advance. Do not surprise your child with requirements that have not been discussed.

6.  Establish little jobs around the house for your child to do. Having jobs to do gives your child a sense of worth and belonging. It also helps your child learn good habits.

7.  **Avoid screen time for your child until age three.** There is evidence that too much screen time inhibits brain development in children under age three. In order to develop normally, children need to be physically active and interact with other people as much as possible.

8.  **Use coloring books so your child learns about colors and about how to hold pencils and pens.** Coloring can stimulate creativity, help develop fine motor skills and be a learning opportunity

9.  **Introduce your child to other children and adults.** Time with other children and other adults helps your child be ready for school.

10. **Encourage your child to play independently with clothes, blocks, pots and pans or other safe household items.** Independent play reduces dependency.

*Adapted from Preparing for Kindergarten.com*

# ENDNOTES

## PREFACE

1. Terry M. Moe, editor, *A Primer on America's Schools* (Stanford: Hoover Institution Press, 2001), 5–6.

2. John Taylor Gatto, *The Underground History of American Education* (New York, Oxford Village Press, 1995), 25.

3. Ibid., 31.

4. https://www.biography.com/people/horace-mann-9397522.

5. New American Academy, "The Prussian-Industrial Model: The Roots of Public Schooling," at webpage http://thenewamericanacademy.org/ index.php/home/our-philosophy-menu/the-prussian-industrial-model.

6. Ibid.

7. Joel Rose, "How to Break Free of Our 19th-Century Factory-Model Education System," *The Atlantic* (May 19, 2012), http://www.theatlantic.com/business/archive/2012/05/how-to-break-free-of-our-19th-century-factory-model-education-system/256881/.

8. Ellwood P. Cubberly, *Public Education in the United States* (Boston: Houghton-Mifflin, 1919), 355.

9. Claudia Goldin, "How America Graduated From High School, 1910–1960," National Bureau of Economic Research, June 1994.

10. Claudia Goldin, "How America Graduated From High School, 1910–1960," National Bureau of Economic Research, June 1994.

11. See "A New Majority: Low Income Students Now a Majority in the Nation's Public Schools," *Research Bulletin, Southern Education Foundation* (January 2015). This is an update of the SEF's 2013 report. http://www.southerneducation.org/getattachment/4ac62e27-5260-47a5-9d02-14896ec3a531/A-New-Majority-2015-Update-Low-Income-Students-Now.aspx.

12. Harold L. Hodgkinson, quoted in Debra Viadero, "South's Schools Pass Milestone on Poverty," *Education Week* (November 7, 2007), 14.

13. Steve Suitts, "A New Majority: Low Income Students Now a Majority in the Nation's Public Schools," *Research Bulletin, Southern Education Foundation* (January 2015), p. 4. The entire bulletin is available at: http://www.southerneducation.org/getattachment/4ac62e27-5260-47a5-9d02-14896ec3a531/A-New-Majority-2015-Update-Low-Income-Students-Now.aspx.

14. Rachel Sheffield and Robert Rector, "The War On Poverty After 50 Years," *Poverty and Inequality* (The Heritage Foundation, September 15, 2014).

## INTRODUCTION

1. Ted Dintersmith, What School Could Be (Princeton University Press, 2018), p. xiii.

2. US News, April 25, 2017.

## 1. THE EXISTING SYSTEM

1. "Condition of College & Career Readiness 2013," http://www.act.org/research/policy-makers/cccr13/readiness1.html.

2. National Assessment of Educational Progress, *The Nation's Report Card, 2013,* Mathematics and Reading, 7.

3. *Education Week,* Children Trends Database, January, 2014, http://www.statisticbrain.com/high-school-dropout-statistics/.

4. Stephanie Banchero, "High-School Graduation Rate Inches Up," *Wall Street Journal,* January 22, 2013.

5. *PISA 2012 Results In Focus: What 15-Year-Olds Know and What They Can Do With What They Know,* OECD 2014, 5, https://www.oecd.org/pisa/keyfindings/pisa-2012-results-overview.pdf.

6. Organization for Economic Cooperation and Development, *OECD Factbook Statistics* (2013), http://www.oecd-ilibrary.org.

7. Tom Carroll, "Education Beats Incarceration," *Education Week* (March 26, 2008), 32.

8. Teach For America, Annual Report, 2015.

9. National Commission on Teaching and America's Future, "No Dream Denied: A Pledge to America's Children, Summary Report," (Washington, DC: NCTAF, 2003), 10.

10. Ibid., 13.

11. "Council of Great City Schools," *Urban Indicator* (Fall 2010), 2.

12. Ibid., 1.

13. National Center for Education Statistics, *Digest of Education Statistics 2015,* Table 601.60. For the United States, the actual average for all states is 178, even though most states show 180 days as their school year. Other countries have similarly lengthened school years, but are not listed for the sake of brevity.

14. Ted Dintersmith, *What Schools Could Be* (Princeton: Princeton University Press, 2018), p. xvi.

## 2. EXTERNAL FACTORS

1. U.S. Department of Health and Human Services, National Center for Health Statistics, "Marriages and Divorces, 1900–2009."

2. U.S. Census Bureau, Statistical Abstract of the United States, 2011, Section 2, "Births, Deaths, Marriages and Divorces."

3. John L. Rury, *Education and Social Change: Contours in the History of American Schooling* (New York: Routledge, 2013, 41.

4. M. W. Sedlak and S. Schlossman, *Who Will Teach? Historical Perspectives on the Changing Appeal of Teaching as a Profession* (Rand Corporation: Santa Monica, CA, 1986), 33.

5. Virginia Historical Society web site: http://www.vahistorical.org/beginnings.black.

6. Nicholas D. Kristof, "Students Over Unions," *New York Times* (September 12, 2012), A31.

7. *U.S. Census Bureau Current Population Survey, 1960–2010,* Annual Social and Economic Supplements.

8.  Michael Turner, "War on Poverty at 50—Despite Trillions Spent, Poverty Won," Cato Institute, January 8, 2014.

9.  U.S. Census Bureau, "Income and Poverty in the United States 2016," Report Number P60, 259.

10.  Terry Moe, *Special Interest: Teachers Unions and America's Public Schools* (Washington, DC: Brookings Institution Press, 2011), 48.

11.  Ibid., 49.

12.  Ibid., 37.

13.  Ibid., 52.

14.  Roger Clegg, "Latest Statistics on Out of Wedlock Births," The Corner, *National Review Online* (October 11, 2013).

15.  Caroline May, "Number of Children Born Out of Wedlock In The U.S. Is Soaring," *Business Insider* (February 12, 2012), 1.

16.  Laurence Steinberg, "Student Beliefs/Character Education," Hoover Institution, 118, http://media.hoover.org/sites/default/files/documents/ 0817928723_117.pdf.

17.  Ibid., 118.

18.  Ibid., 120

## 3. The Mission of School

1.  Department of Labor, *Secretary's Report on Necessary Skills* (1992).

2.  Kenneth Labich, "What Our Kids Must Learn," *Fortune Magazine* (January 27, 1992), 64–66.

3.  Howard Gardner, *Globalization: Culture and Education in the New Millennium* (Berkeley: University of California Press, 2004), 23–2

4.  David Brooks, *The Social Animal* (New York: Random House, 2011), 8.

5.  Willard R. Daggett, "School Reform," International Center for Leadership in Education, Inc. (1998), 2, http://www.arkansased.org/public/userfiles/ Learning_Services/Curriculum%20and%20Instruction/Char%20Cent%20Teach/dagget.pdf.

6.  Lawrence W. Reed, "Are We Rome?" (1st printing; Atlanta: Foundation for Economic Education, 2015), 5. The pdf can be downloaded from https://fee.org/resources/are-we-rome-by-lawrence-w-reed/.

7.  David Brooks, *The Social Animal* (New York: Random House, 2011), 14.

8.  Department of Labor, "Raising Standards for American Education" (1992), http://www.scribd.com/doc/143404039/National-Council-On-Education-Standards-and-Testing-Raising-Standards-for-American-Education.

9.  Ibid., 2.

10.  Amanda Ripley, *The Smartest Kids in the World* (New York: Simon and Schuster, 2013), 120.

11.  Ibid., 123.

## 4. Unions and Change

1.  Terry Moe, "The Staggering Power of Teachers' Unions," *Hoover Digest* no. 3 (2011), 94, http://www.hoover.org/research/staggering-power-teachers-unions.

2. Joel Klein, "The Failure of American Schools," *The Atlantic Monthly* (June, 2011), 2, http://www.theatlantic.com/magazine/archive/2011/06/the-failure-of-american-schools/308497/.

3. https://en.wikipedia.org/wiki/ United_Automobile_Workers.

4. "Teacher Contracts: Restoring the Balance," Executive Summary, *The Education Partnership* (March 2005), 7.

5. Ibid., 7.

6. Terry Moe, "The Staggering Power of Teachers' Unions," *Hoover Digest* 3 (Summer 2011), 94, http://www.hoover.org/research/staggering-power-teachers-unions.

7. Ibid.

8. Terry Moe, *Special Interest: Teachers Unions and America's Public Schools* (Washington, DC: Brookings Institution Press, 2011), 8.

9. Ibid., 283.

10. James Wigderson, "Wisconsin Teachers Union Membership Plummets Since Act 10," Watchdog.org, June 21, 2016.

## 5. Teaching

1. "How to Be Top," *The Economist* (October 20, 2007), 80.

2. Kati Haycock, "Closing the Achievement Gap," *Educational Leadership* (March 2001).

3. "Good Teaching Matters—How Well-Qualified Teachers Can Close the Gap," *Thinking K–16* 3, no. 2 (Washington, DC: Education Trust, 1998), 3–5.

4. Jay P. Greene, "The Cost of Remedial Education: How Much Michigan Pays When Students Fail to Learn Basic Skills" (Midland, MI: MacKinac Center for Public Policy, 2003), 3.

5. The Teaching Commission, "Teaching At Risk, A Call to Action" (2004), 12.

6. Ibid. 10.

7. "Joint Statement from Twelve Education Organizations on the U.S. Department of Education's Teacher Preparation Regulation" (April 25, 2014), http://www.edtrust.org/dc/press-room/news/joint-statement-from-twelve-education-organizations-on-the-us-department-of-educa.

8. Education Trust, "Good Teaching Matters—How Well-Qualified Teachers Can Close the Gap," *Thinking K–16* 3, no. 2 (Washington, DC: Education Trust, 1998), 4.

9. The Teaching Commission, "Teaching at Risk: A Call to Action" (2004), 19.

10. National Commission on Teaching and America's Future, "No Dream Denied: Pledge to America's Children, Summary Report" (Washington, DC: NCTAF, 2003), 13.

11. Grover Whitehurst, "Raising Student Achievement: The Evidence of High Quality Teaching," remarks at STEP 2002 Summer Conference (June 11, 2002).

12. The Teaching Commission, "Teaching At Risk: A Call to Action" (2004), 18.

13. Richard F. Elmore, "Breaking the Cartel," *Phi Delta Kappan* (March 2006), 517, http://www.kappanmagazine.org/content/87/7/517.abstract.

14. Arthur Levine, *Educating School Teachers* (Washington, DC: Education Schools Project, 2006).

15. Ibid., 1.

16. Ibid., 4.

17. The Teaching Commission, "Teaching at Risk: A Call to Action" (2004), 17.

18. U.S. Department of Education, Office of Policy Planning and Innovation, "Meeting the Highly Qualified Teachers Challenge: The Secretary's Second Annual Report on Teacher Quality" (Washington, DC, 2003), 46.

19. Lawrence Baines, "The Highly Qualified Teacher Lie," *Education Week*, March 8, 2017, 24.

20. David W. Kirkpatrick, Alexis de Tocqueville Institution, "Teacher Certification Procedures are a Joke!" (June, 2000), 1, http://www.schoolreport.com/schoolreport/articles/certification_joke_6_00.htm.

21. D. R. Sterling, "The Teacher Shortage: National Trends for Science and Mathematics," *Journal of Mathematics and Science* 7 (2004), 85–96, http://www.math.vcu.edu/g1/journal/Journal7/Part%20I/Sterling.html.

22. Ibid. 85–96.

23. Norm R. Augustine, "Rising above the Gathering Storm," Statement before the Committee on Science, U.S. House of Representatives (October 20, 2005).

24. Public Agenda, "An Assessment of Survey Data on Attitudes about Teaching, Including the Views of Parents, Administrators, Teachers and the General Public," compiled for The Teaching Commission, 20.

25. "The Loss of Our Faculties," *Society for Quality Education* (June 7, 2011), http://www.societyforqualityeducation.org/index.php/blog/the-loss-of-our-faculties.

26. "Teachers Want to Lead Their Profession's Transformation," *Education Week* (February 8, 2012), 24, http://www.edweek.org/ew/articles/2012/ 02/08/20debose.h31.html.

27. Robert Herbold, President's Council of Advisors on Science and Technology, "K–12 Establishment is Putting America's Industrial Leadership at Risk," speech on May 25, 2004, Seattle, Washington, http://www.freerepublic.com/focus/f-news/1341254/posts.

28. TNTP web site.

29. Amanda Ripley, *The Smartest Kids in the World* (New York: Simon and Schuster, 2013), 89.

30. Ibid.

31. Based upon a personal study of the Singapore education system and discussions with leaders of the Singapore Education Ministry, 2016.

32. Byron Auguste, Paul Kinn, and Matt Miller, "Closing the talent gap: Attacting and retaining top third graduates to a career in teaching," McKinsey & Co. (September 2010), 1, http://mckinseyonsociety.com/closing-the-talent-gap/.

33. Amanda Ripley, *The Smartest Kids*, 89.

34. Betty Wallace and William Graves, *The Poisoned Apple* (New York: St. Martin's Press, 1995), 37.

35. William Stevenson and James W. Stigler, *The Learning Gap* (New York: Summit Books, 1992), 175.

36. "Lessons Learned," *Public Agenda* 1 (2007), 25, http://www.publicagenda.org/files/lessons_learned_1.pdf.

37. Allan Odden, "Rewarding Expertise," *Education Next* 1, no. 1 (Spring 2001), http://educationnext.org/rewarding-expertise/.

38. The above numbers are based upon Seattle, but they are comparable for urban districts across the country. http://www.k12.wa.us/safs/PUB/PER/ 1718/tbl19.pdf.

39. National Center for Education Statistics, *Digest of Education Statistics*, 2017, Table 211.60.

40. Ibid

## 6. LEADERSHIP

1. Gregory F. Branch, Eric A. Hanushek, and Steven G. Rivkin, "School Leaders Matter," *Education Next* 13, no. 1 (Winter 2013), http://educationnext.org/school-leaders-matter/.

2. "How Leadership Improves Student Learning," *Wallace Foundation* (September 2004), 5.

3. Richard Elmore, *School Reform from the Inside Out: Policies, Practices and Performance* (Cambridge, MA: Harvard Education Press, 2004), 59.

4. Ibid., 60.

## 7. GOVERNANCE

1. National Center for Education Statistics, *Digest of Education Statistics*, 2012 Tables and Figures, Table 98.

2. David Kirkpatrick, "The Superintendency: Neither Inevitable nor Necessary," *Free Republic*, http://www.freerepublic.com/focus/f-news/1325624/posts.

3. "Council of Great City Schools," *Urban Indicator* (Fall 2010), 2.

4. Ibid.

## 8. GROUP VERSUS INDIVIDUALIZED LEARNING

1. Amanda Ripley, *The Smartest Kids in the World* (New York: Simon and Schuster, 2013), 120.

2. "Not in School and Not Working," *Education News* (October 25, 2013), 2.

3. Ibid., 3.

## 9. A LONGER DAY/YEAR AND TIME VERSUS ACHIEVEMENT

1. Betty Wallace and William Graves, *The Poisoned Apple* (New York: St. Martin's Press, 1995), 23–24.

2. "Michigan Initiative Scraps Grade Levels and Letter Grades," *Education Week* (October 3, 2012), 12.

3. Ibid., 12.

## 10. TECHNOLOGY

1. Alexander Russo, "Notable Education Stories," *The Atlantic*, December 5, 2013, p. 6.

2. Lillian Pace, "A Pathway for the Future of Education," *Education Week* (September 25, 2013), 32.

3. Sean Cavanagh, "District Officials Eye Blended Learning, With Cautionary Lessons in Mind," *Education Week Online* (November 5, 2013), http://www.edweek.org/ew/articles/2013/11/06/ 11techtrends.h33.html.

4. Howard Blume, "Mixed Reaction to iPad Rollout From L.A. Teachers and Administrators," *Los Angeles Times*, December 2, 2013, http://www.latimes.com/local/la-me-ipads-survey-20131202-story.html.

5. http://www.coursera.org.

6. http://www.khanacademy.org.

7. Irene Middleman, Thomas, "Sal Khan Is a Can-Do Guy," *The Costco Connection* (August 2013), p. 32, http://www.costcoconnection.com/connection/201308?article_id=1235220&pg=35#pg35.

8. http://www.khanacademy.org.

9. Tony Wagner, *The Global Achievement Gap* (New York: Basic Books, 2008), 125.

10. Ted Dintersmith, *What School Could Be: Insights and Inspiration from Teachers across America* (Princeton University Press, 2018), 63–64.

11. Liv Finne, "Review of Digital Leaning in Private Schools and Public Charter Schools," Washington Policy Center (November 3, 2013), http://www.washingtonpolicy.org/publications/notes/review-digital-learning-private-schools-and-public-charter-schools.

## 11. CHOICE, VOUCHERS AND CHARTERS

1. Orleans Parish Schools: http://www.nops.k12.la.us.

2. Friends of Choice in Urban Schools: http://www.focusdc.org.

3. New Orleans Business Alliance, "New Orleans High School Graduation Rate Outperforms U.S.," June 18, 2013, http://nolaba.org/new-orleans-high-school-grad-rate-outperforms-us/.

## 12. BRAIN DEVELOPMENT AND EARLY CHILDHOOD EDUCATION

1. Thomas Nagel, *Mind and Cosmos* (New York: Oxford University Press, 2012), 29-33.

2. "Baby Brain Map," *Zero to Three*, http://www.zerotothree.org/child-development/brain-development/baby-brain-map.html.

3. Ibid.

4. Bruce Perry and John Marceilus, "Personal Perspective: The Time Is Now," http://www.scholastic.com/teachers/article/personal-perspective-time-now.

5. Jack P. Shonkoff, "The Science of Early Childhood Development," Concept Paper for the Board of Directors of Thrive by Five (July 2006), 9.

6. Patricia Kuhn, "The Linguistic Genius of Babies," *TEDxRainier* (October, 2010), http://ilabs.washington.edu/i-labs-news/dr-kuhls-ted-talk-linguistic-genius-of-babies.

7. Jack P. Shonkoff and Deborah A. Phillips, eds., *From Neurons to Neighborhoods: The Science of Early Childhood Development* (Washington, DC: National Academy Press, 2000), 8.

8. Betty Hart and Todd R. Risley, "Meaningful Differences in Everyday Experience of Young American Children," http://www.strategiesforchildren.org/researchbriefs.html.

9. John Medina, *Brain Rules: 12 Principles for Surviving and Thriving at Work, Home, and School* (Seattle: Pear Press, 2008), 186.

10. Ibid., 190.

11. Ibid., 199.

12. "Emotional Literacy: Rethinking Problem Behavior in Preschool," in *A Fair Start: Equity and Excellence in Early Childhood Education*, Volume 6 of *Research that Matters* (Seattle: University of Washington, 2008), 5. See https://flipflashpages.uniflip.com/3/93263/331853/pub/html5.html.

13. Jack P. Shonkoff and Deborah A. Phillips, eds., *From Neurons to Neighborhoods: The Science of Early Childhood Development* (Washington, DC: National Academy Press, 2000), 10.

14. Ibid., 14.

15. Lawrence J. Schweinhart, president, High/Scope Educational Research Foundation, *Lifetime Effects: The High/Scope Perry Preschool Study Through Age 40* (Ypsilanti, Mich: High/Scope Press, 2005).

## 13. A Call to Action

1. U.S. National Commission on Excellence in Education, *A Nation At Risk* (Washington, DC: National Commission on Excellence in Education, 1983), 1.

2. Arthur Levine, "The Plight of Teachers' Unions," *Education Week* 32:30 (May 8, 2013), 36.

3. Marion Brady, "What's Worth Learning," *Information Age Publishing* (2013), vii.

4. Ibid., 19.

5. Jeb Bush, "Speech to the National Education Summit," *Foundation for Excellence in Education* (October 17, 2013), http://excelined.org/downloads/remarks-by-governor-jeb-bush-at-2013-national-summit-on-education-reform_october-17-2013/.

6. Geneviève DiBose, Claire Jellinek, et al., "Teachers Want to Lead Their Profession's Transformation," *Education Week* (February 8, 2012), http://www.edweek.org/ew/articles/2012/02/08/20debose.h31.html.

7. Tony Wagner, *The Global Achievement Gap* (New York: Basic Books, 2008), 243.

8. Ibid., 242.

9. Barry E. Stern, "ACT Study Shows Little Progress in Preparing High School Graduates for College and Careers," *Education News* (September 17, 2010), http://www.education-news.org/ed_reports/99898.html.

10. "Good Governance Starts and Ends with Strong Schools," *Center for Reinventing Public Education Blog* (September 17, 2013), http://www.crpe.org/thelens/good-governance-starts-and-ends-strong-schools.

11. "Uncommon Schools Wins Broad Prize for Charter Schools," *Broad Foundation* (July 2, 2013), http://www.broadprize.org/news/61.html.

## 14. The Game Plan

1. 165. Two exceptions to this statement are Massachusetts and the District of Columbia. In both cases, there has been very strong leadership at the Gubernatorial and Legislative level (Massachusetts) or at the Mayoral and Chancellor's level (DC). Those conditions have allowed significant change to occur without having "Right-to-Work" legislation in place.

2. Nithin Iyengar, Kate Lewis-Lamonica, and Mike Perigo, "Should Donors Invest in School Districts?" *Philanthropy*, Fall, 2017, 51.

# INDEX

New Schools Venture Fund, 20
New York City Public Schools, 47, 89
Nielsen, Don, 31
Nielsen, Sandy, 22
Nutley, Erik, 22
Nuxol, Carla, 20

**O**
Olchefske, Joseph, 46
Opportunity Nation, 158
Oschefsky, Joseph, 21

**P**
Pace, Lillian, 174
Paige, Rod, 20, 136
Parent, role of, 83
Pasquarella, Robin, 21
Pay of teachers, 229
Payzant, Tom, 19
Perot, Ross, 20
Perry, Bruce, 194
Perry Preschool Project, 201–202
Petersen, Barbara, 21
Phillips, Vicki, 22
Pianta, Bob, 20
Pianta, Robert, 21
*Poisoned Apple, The*, 38, 124, 168
Popham, W. James, 116
Poverty, 13
Preschool, 197–198, 199–202
Preston, Michael, 21
Principal certification, 43
Principal, leadership by, 222–223
Promotion by self-selection, 135
Public Agenda, 116
*Public Education in the United States*

(1919), 11
Public Education Leadership Program (PELP), 21
Public Education Leadership Project (PELP), 141

**R**
Recovery School District (RSD), 188
Reed, Lawrence W., 78
Rhee, Michelle, 19, 98
Right to work law, 88, 100
Right-to-Work legislation, 218
Riley, Mike, 21
Rios, Francisco, 20
Ripley, Amanda, 84
Risley, Todd R., 195
Rivkin, Steven G., 133
Roe, Ellen, 21
Romer, Roy, 20
Rosenstock, Larry, 20
Russo, Alexander, 173

**S**
Salick, Anna, 22
SAT score, 110, 114
Schaad-Lamphere, Barbara, 21
Schmitt, Sue, 21
Schnur, John, 22
School
  accreditation, 115
  after WWII, 55–57
  before WWII, 55–57
  charter, 188–190, 219
  high-tech, 174
  in Colonial America, 9
  innovation in, 219
  Innovation Zone, 220
  mission of, 73, 241